HUNGRY LIGHTNING

hungry
lightning

Notes of a Woman
Anthropologist in Venezuela

Pei-Lin Yu

UNIVERSITY OF NEW MEXICO PRESS | ALBUQUERQUE

© 1997 by the University of New Mexico Press

Illustrations © 1997 by Pei-Lin Yu

Second paperbound printing, 1998

Library of Congress Cataloging-in-Publication Data

Yu, Pei-Lin, 1964–

Hungry lightning : notes of a woman anthropologist in Venezuela

Pei-Lin Yu—first edition

p. cm.

ISBN 0–8263–1807–x (pbk.)

1. Yu, Pei-Lin, 1964.

2. Women anthropologists—Venezuela—Biography

3.Yaruro Indians—Social life and customs

4. Ethnology—Field work

I. Title

GN21.Y8A3 1997 97–4845

306'.902 — DC21

CIP

No sooner are such people known, or guessed at, than
their strangeness drops away, and one might as well have
stayed in one's own village. Or if . . . their strangeness
remained intact, then it was no good to me, for I could
not even begin to analyse it.

They were as close to me as an image seen in a looking-
glass: I could touch, but not understand them.
Jean-Claude Levi-Strauss, *Tristes Tropiques*

Without zest in the face of hardship, travel writing
soon becomes little more than a record of misery.
Larry McMurtry in his Introduction to George Kennan's
Tent Life in Siberia

When I get hungry enough, then killing and falling
are dancing, too.
Maxine Hong Kingston, *The Woman Warrior*

If you know you have an allergy to sea snake venom,
perhaps drunken diving for poison sea snakes is not for you.
Tim Cahill, *A Wolverine is Eating My Leg*

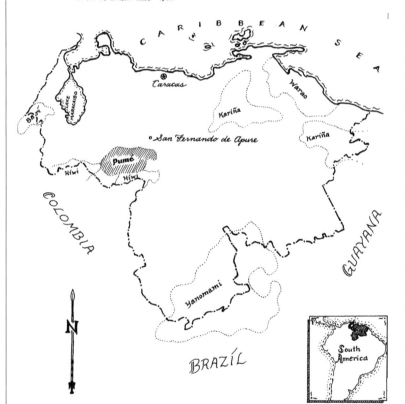

Venezuela

With geographic
distributions of
selected ethnographic
groups

SCALE

0   100   200   300   400 Km.

▭ = Modern boundary
     of ethnographic group

• After R. Lizarralde 1982

C A R I B B E A N   S E A

⊕ Caracas

Warao

BARÍ

LAGO DE MARACAIBO

Kariña

○ San Fernando de Apure

Kariña

Pumé

Híwi   Híwi

COLOMBIA

GUAYANA

N

Yanomami

BRAZÍL

South America

Contents

Preface

Hungry Lightning is an informal, personal account of events that occurred during anthropological research on the Pumé Indians of Venezuela in the years 1992–1993. For the privacy of the Pumé and their neighbors, I have changed local place names in the text. No scientific data are presented in this work. For scientific findings related to this research project, please see Russell D. Greaves's doctoral dissertation, entitled "Ethnoarchaeological investigation of subsistence mobility, resource targeting, and technological organization among Pumé foragers of Venezuela" (University of New Mexico, 1997).

This book could not have been written without the help of hundreds of people. I thank you all, and I'd like to personally acknowledge some of you here:

—To the Pumé of Doro Aná, for their humor, hospitality, kindness, family feeling, and tolerance in the face of constant invasions of privacy into their everyday lives. With their help, I learned a great deal about how people organize their lives and the world around them. The Pumé fed our research group, taught us their language, built houses for us, carried our gear, helped us survive, and ultimately adopted us as family. I owe them a debt of gratitude that is impossible to describe.

—To Dr. Russell (Rusty) Greaves, for helping me reach new levels of understanding in the field of anthropology, and for opening up emotional vistas I was previously unaware of. As my constant companion for two years in the field and three more at home, he nourishes my hunger for knowledge in an atmosphere of challenge, insight, and humor. Dr. Greaves's dissertation provides a scholarly treatment of this project.

—To my family, who have encouraged me in a field whose rewards are not always apparent. My mother and father lent us money to treat my illnesses in the field, and I was able to recuperate and continue to collect information vital to the project due to their understanding, resourcefulness, and generosity in time of need.

—To the Aguilar family, for their hospitality in the *llanos*. They fed us enormous meals, transported us and our gear many times in and out of town, treated us with home remedies in times of illness, and were staunch friends in times of peace, crisis, or merrymaking.

—To Dr. Esteban Tillet, for training me in ethnobotanical collection and recording methods. All plants used culturally by the Pumé that were collected by myself and by Dr. Ted Gragson are curated at the Central University of Venezuela under Dr. Tillett's care.

—To Dr. Roberto Lizarralde, also of the Central University of Venezuela, for his hospitality in Caracas and for his helpful information on the Doro Aná Pumé, based on many years of anthropological fieldwork in the Doro Aná area.

—To Dr. Otto Fornés and his wife Margarita, who provided invaluable assistance in navigating the permitting system in Venezuela. Dr. and Mrs. Fornés are also owed many thanks for rescuing, feeding, and housing me during travel emergencies.

—To José Rafael Pernía, his sister Flor Chavez, and her family, for their hospitality in Caracas and their kind help in the frenzy of travel planning.

—To Gemma Orobitg, for her moral support, professiona[l] vice, and her very kind loan of space in her apartment durii[ng] hectic stay in Caracas.

—To Dr. Theodore Gragson, whose dissertation based on [a]thropological fieldwork with the Doro Aná Pumé in 1987 a[nd] 1988 provided vital information for this book. The first Nor[th] Americans to visit the Doro Aná Pumé, Dr. Gragson and his wi[fe] Gay became respected members of the Pumé family, and our su[b]sequent rapid adoption by the group was facilitated by the hig[h] regard the Pumé had for them.

—To Dr. Charles (Chuck) Hilton, for his friendship, insights, and logistical help during his stay with us at Doro Aná. Dr. Hilton's dissertation on Pumé locomotion is listed in the section on Further Reading.

—To Direccion Asunto Indígenas (Caracas) and the Oficina Regional Asunto Indígenas (San Fernando de Apure), for help with permitting procedures, numerous rides to the field, and donated supplies.

—To the University of New Mexico Anthropology Department, which fostered me through my undergraduate years, and provided Rusty Greaves with the intellectual environment that led to the formulation of the Pumé Ethnoarchaeological Project. Rusty's doctoral dissertation committee, Dr. Lewis Binford, Dr. Hillard Kaplan, and Dr. Erik Trinkaus at the University of New Mexico, and Dr. George Frison at the University of Wyoming, contributed toward the project's design.

—To Dr. Barry Kues, staunch correspondent and true friend, whose timely advocacy brought this book to publication.

A Guide to Pronunciation

In this book, I have written the Pumé language in a form that will be easily understood by American English speakers. Vowels are pronounced similarly to Latin or Spanish:

a = ah,
e = eh,
i = ee,
o = oh,
u = ooh

The ñ that is familiar in Spanish I have written more literally as -ny in Pumé. Most Pumé words are accented or stressed on the last syllable, which is indicated by an accent (as in Pumé) in the text.

For pronunciation of the Spanish terms, consult a Spanish grammar guide or dictionary.

HUNGRY LIGHTNING

Prologue

In which I get a letter;

I sign my life away

for two years;

I set off for Venezuela

and parts unknown

12/10/90 *"HELL YES!"* Pressing hard, I underlined the capital letters three times. "Where do I sign?" Later, walking through the snow to the mailbox, I wondered what exactly I'd agreed to.

An intriguing letter had arrived at my house in Oregon a few days earlier. It was from a friend of mine, Rusty Greaves, a Ph.D. candidate at the University of New Mexico. In his letter, Rusty described the project he was working on to earn his doctorate in anthropology: he was going to live with and study a group of hunter-gatherer Indians, called the Pumé, in South America. The information he collected would later be used in studies of archaeological sites, to see if a living people's way of life could help shed light on the lives of ancient hunter-gatherers.

I was happy for him; it sounded deliciously exciting. Just the country's name, "Venezuela," conjured up images of steaming cloud-forests filled with brilliantly colored birds flashing through the trees and spiders the size of dinner plates lurking in the undergrowth. Or of limitless golden grasslands under hot blue skies, stalked by the jaguars and giant anteaters . . .

One thing the project lacked, Rusty wrote, was a field assistant. He needed a woman researcher to work with the Indian women, as few studies of hunter-gatherer women exist in the anthropological literature. All expenses would be covered, but there would be no salary. The project would last more than eighteen months. I could expect to live under the most difficult, trying field conditions imaginable, including hunger, disease, and, of course, hard work. The bugs were guaranteed to drive me insane. Would I be interested?

My job as an archaeologist for the Forest Service provided steady, well-paid work but was uninspiring. After three years I already felt myself slipping into the mindless defensiveness of a government employee; I found myself in tiny, smoky Oregon bars, justifying over cheap beer the spending on archaeology of American tax dollars. After thinking over Rusty's proposition for a day or two, I sent him my cautious reply.

2/14/92 More than a year later the plane disgorged us amid a swirl of passengers into the echoing pandemonium of the Caracas airport. It was a cool and windy night, but we had no chance to enjoy it; the second we appeared in the terminal with our mountain of baggage, a gang of nine men pounced on us like vultures. They jostled each other, yelling, for the privilege of grabbing our big military duffel bags.

Somehow we ended up in a beat-up Chevy van whose interior was covered floor to ceiling in orange shag rug. Our bags were piled in back, and an unctuously smiling driver sat in front, holding out his hand and demanding an outrageous price to take us into town. We had no choice. Rusty peeled off the bills, and we joined the stream of nighttime traffic on the dark highway into the capital.

That is where my journal begins. For the next year and a half, it was to be my constant companion and my sanity's savior, ultimately expanding to fill two large notebooks smeared with fish juice, bloodstains, smashed mosquitoes, baby drool, and the furtive scribbles of naughty children. As I sit here now and puzzle over my handwriting, the smells, colors, noises and tastes, the frustration, terror, joy and confusion shout up at me from the wrinkled pages.

Cities and Towns

FEBRUARY–APRIL 1992

In which we acquaint ourselves with

the great capital and discover each other;

Carnaval street madness; hostile bureaucrats;

a terrifying political demonstration;

an enchanting little cowtown;

the sunbaked plain

2/15/92   Our hotel is located in the center of Caracas, the four-hundred-year-old sprawling capital of Venezuela. Since we're on the eighth floor, the cool breezes that pour down from the forested hills surrounding the city wash through our room at night. Today Rusty showed me around the Caracas. Aside from the bullet-pock-marked presidential palace and soldiers on streetcorners armed with submachine guns and tear-gas canisters, there are few signs of the violence that erupted here ten days ago, when an attempted military coup d'etat claimed many lives. The failed coup, which nearly put an end to our plans to come here, is engraved on the faces of the people on the street, whose expressions are tense and, in some cases, seem to reveal a schoolchild's complicity.

Seeking refuge from the hot, crowded streets, we sat in a quiet cafe, outside under an umbrella. My first meal here was roast chicken, fried plantains, rice, and a lovely drink called a *batido,* made from whipped fresh pineapple, ice, and milk. I am now fervently wishing I'd taken Spanish classes; my inadequate grasp of the language allows me only to identify isolated words, like flashes of light in the racket of conversation. We still aren't used to the heat, and after walking all afternoon we stopped, sweat-drenched, to gulp down cold, clear, sweet coconut milk straight out of the shell at a street vendor's stand. Now it's night again and the noises of the city (car alarms, water running in the gutter, a woman screaming, strange bird calls) float companionably up to our window.

2/16/92   The inevitable has happened between Rusty and me. We've known each other off and on for years, and I must admit I anticipated it, but this is earlier and more shocking than I expected. . . . Oh well, Caracas is a town full of contented lovers in all shapes, sizes, colors, and ages. Rusty and I fit in easily with the other couples walking or sitting entwined in the streets and parks.

2/17/92   We hit the streets early today to begin getting our government paperwork in order. Since Rusty was here in 1990 for

eight months, he's already been through the permitting procedures for scientific work, but it looks like we may have to do it all
over again. I hope our money holds out; this hotel, although one
of the cheapest we could find, is more than we can afford for long.

Walking the streets, I notice that Venezuelan women resemble
chicana women to the second power. They loudly advertise themselves in bright miniskirts or skin-tight jeans worn with spike heels.
The variety of faces, shapes, and colors is astounding. Venezuelans describe themselves as *cafe con leche,* or coffee with cream, to
describe skin tones that ranges from deep, velvety black to bronze
to glowing gold. It's a shame the women wear so much makeup,
covering up their huge brown eyes and satiny lashes with eye-
shadow and coats of mascara. Their full lips are hidden behind
neon red or pink lipstick, and huge Italianate earrings dangle to
just above their shoulders. I don't know how Venezuelan men are
able to function, what with billboards, TV, and live women hurling sex at them all day long.

2/28/92   Week after week Rusty and I swim against the endless
current of government offices, arguing politely in Spanish with bored
or actively hostile officials: "Why do you want to work with the
Indians? *Our* scientists have already done all this." (I am eyed
with disapproval.) "Why didn't you hire a Venezuelan for an assistant?" (Simulated surprise.) "What d'you mean, no one here is
interested? . . . Anyway, we can't possibly rush your application. . . .
Yes, at least eight weeks. . . . This needs to be signed by a lawyer
and notarized. . . . That will be 500 bolívares, please. . . . Why don't
you go to the beach, have a good time? . . . He isn't here, come back
tomorrow, early. . . . Well, try again Monday. Early."

In colorful relief to our frustrations, Carnaval, the rowdy pre-
lude to Holy Week, starts this weekend. The streets are bright
with children in costume: pirates, harem girls, strawberries, dal-
matian dogs, and little soldiers dressed up like Lt. Hugo Chavez,
the imprisoned leader of the recent unsuccessful military coup.

The very young children wear their costumes with tolerant dignity, humoring adults who want to show them off. Bigger kids amuse themselves by flinging handfuls of confetti into each others' eyes or squirting waterguns at unwary grownups.

The adults drink beer, flirt, admire each others' children, struggle to keep track of their own, and pursue the endless business of buying and selling on the crowded streets. A big band of Caribbean drummers, all wearing brilliant blue shirts, winds through the mayhem like a giant snake, the leader blowing a shrill whistle to maintain the brassy, sexy beat. The crowd drops everything and surges to the rhythm, laughing, strangers dancing with each other.

3/10/92 Day by day the tropical sun pummels the huge plants of the city, which nod wisely as people and animals swirl around them. The crumbling concrete buildings, decrepit after only twenty or thirty years, peer out through masks of graffiti and grime. Nearly half the population of this country has poured into the capital city in the last ten years, and they are now living on top of each other in horrible slums called *rancheros,* while the little farms and ranches sag quietly into ruin in the abandoned countryside.

There are millions of homeless beggars of all ages and sexes here, who have somehow managed to keep hold of their humor and pride. Rusty tells me that once a young man approached him, aggressively begging for money, and Rusty replied evasively that he didn't speak Spanish, using the word *español.* The beggar drew himself up to his full height and wagged an admonitory finger in Rusty's face: "Listen, here in South America we don't use that word! It's *castellano,* chico!"

The young people of Caracas are recklessly optimistic, childlike. The flood of images newly available to them via North American posters, movies, radio, and cable television accelerates their craving for bright, cheap objects, things that promise sex, money, big muscles, a small waist, a new car. There is a starved, self-devouring brilliance to popular culture here, like a terminal fever. People who live in the shadow of poverty, disease, and political upheaval don't look to a rosy future for release: *now* is everything!

3/11/92   At about 9:30 last night I sat slumped in a chair, sulking. We've been getting nowhere with the permits, and our money, supposed to last us eighteen months, is running out like blood in this expensive city. The sound of a wooden spoon beating rhythmically on a tin pot brought me out of my funk. I smiled; a noisy family lives below, and I enjoy listening to the mother roaring at her kids. Someone else began banging on a pot. Then someone else. Suddenly the whole city was echoing with the tinny sounds of spoons on pots. As Rusty and I looked at each other, a big gun exploded somewhere near the presidential palace. Smaller guns began to pop sharply in the streets, some nearby.

"Could it be another coup attempt?" I asked Rusty. "Hell if I know," he answered tensely. "Let's get away from the window." Sweating, we doused the lights, hurried into the bathroom, shut the door, and sat huddled together in the bathtub, hoping it would protect us from stray bullets. The noise built to a crescendo with yells and screams, and I pictured soldiers kicking our door down and dragging us off to be questioned as foreign agitators . . .

As the minutes dragged by, the suspense was agonizing, and I was having difficulty breathing. In the uprising five weeks before over a hundred people, most of them bystanders, were killed. Without having to be asked, Rusty crawled on his hands and knees to the refrigerator, got the beer, and slithered back to the tub, where we sat in the dark holding hands and getting drunk.

In the papers this morning they called the disturbance a *"cacerolización."* I'm guessing that the verb *caceroler* means to beat on a casserole dish with any handy implement to express sol-

idarity with antigovernment forces. Maybe the guns were just for emphasis.

4/10/92   Permits in hand at last, we fled Caracas and landed yesterday at the tiny airport in San Fernando, a small ranching town in south-central Venezuela. As we stepped off the little plane, the heat thudded into us like a giant metallic fist. Unlike Caracas, which is cooled by the winds off the hills, San Fernando sits baking on the flat immensity of the plain. The dry season heat is incredible, the kind that squeezes your eyes right out of their sockets.

This part of Venezuela is a vast grassy plain that is called *los llanos*, or the plains, by the Spanish. Only a few meters above sea level, it is nearly flat with several large rivers flowing east to drain into the mighty Orinoco, which in turn empties into the Atlantic Ocean hundreds of miles to the northeast. Each river has a shawl of lush green forest along its banks, and from the air the rivers look like sinuous green worms winding their way through the golden green velvet grassland.

It's exciting and unnerving to be at our last stopping-point before heading for Pumé Indian territory. We have a few days to shop for presents for them, and we've been sweating our way through the tiny, winding streets lugging buckets, shovels, and other necessities back to the hotel. The crumbling adobe buildings with beautiful Italian wrought-iron grilles bake in the sun, giving off a sweet smell of mud and age. I like this town.

San Fernando's crowning glory is a giant fountain at the north end of town. It consists of a huge concrete bowl engraved with interlocking geometric patterns, inlaid with stained glass, and supported on the upraised tails of enormous, toothy concrete crocodiles. Each croc is in turn supported by horns of plenty under each forepaw, and these are overflowing with fruit and flowers. Between *these* are cows' heads on piles of more fruit and flowers. The whole thing is lovingly coated in bright enamel paint, and at night the water soars up, stained by colored lights. Evenings, Rusty and I like to walk over and contemplate this lovely absurdity glowing like a jewel in the darkening plaza.

THE PUMÉ IN THEIR
DRY SEASON CAMP

APRIL–MAY 1992

In which we ride across the great plain;

I meet the Pumé; my first all-night dance;

we move into our Pumé house; a terrible injury;

I struggle with the Pumé tongue; I eat my first

palm-grub; I meet nearby ranchers; I go on my

first gathering trips with the women; fishing

and fish poisoning; fish mud stew; Dori

4/14/92   It took us all day riding on the back of an Indian Affairs Bureau truck to reach our first Pumé community, a small town called Chenchenita. Our trip was hot, jolting, and dusty, but enlivened by the beauty of the landscape; we drove under a brilliant turquoise sky through the grasslands, occasionally skirting shifting, ivory-colored sand dunes and crossing small, wooded creeks whose deep shade seemed like night after the glare of the sun.

Caymans (South American crocodiles) and big turtles sunned themselves lazily in the mud on the side of the dirt road, keeping company with swirling, chattering flocks of birds. Glossy blue-black cormorants, snowy white egrets and storks, caracaras with white crests, cruel hooked beaks and crazy red eyes, and ibises with downward-curving beaks like crescent moons jostled each other in the trees and ponds. The ibis, a bird familiar to me from ancient Egyptian art, comes in colors ranging from dark green to black to white to brilliant scarlet.

The driver was a talkative man who gestured as he steered around breathtaking potholes. While he told me what to do if I came across a jaguar ("Don't *ever* freeze! Just run for your gun! . . . You guys don't even *have* a gun??"), it finally hit me like a thunderclap: My god, I'm really in South America. I'm going to live here for the next year and a half.

We spent the night in the tiny hamlet of Chenchenita. After hours of struggling like a fish in the netlike hammock that is to be my bed, I trudged into the thin early morning sunlight to find Rusty talking with an older Pumé man named Cesar, who volunteered to show us where our community (called Doro Aná, or "Big Creek," in the Pumé language) is currently located. We piled onto the truck, and while he shouted instructions to the driver, we crossed hill after gentle hill, the grass blowing in the cool wind.

We passed an abandoned village—a scatter of upright poles, a couple of scruffy thatched huts, a few empty gourd shells. Suddenly, we topped a rise and we could see them. A crowd of people stood amid a cluster of small shelters of branches and thatch, watching us approach. My heart pounded as if it would burst from my chest; I couldn't breathe.

The truck groaned to a stop in a cloud of dust, and we jumped stiffly off the back. The Pumé stood by quietly as our bags were thrown from the truck. Their skin, hair, and clothes were uniformly gray from dust and wear. I stared hard at my toes, at the bags, at the little branch shelters, at anything but their curious eyes, sucking at me like little vacuums.

A tiny old woman broke the spell, yanking on my sleeve and talking to me earnestly in a high voice. Her wrinkled hands waved at people in the crowd, who shuffled their feet self-consciously. Of course, I couldn't understand a word she said. I waved goodbye weakly to the truck as it rattled off in another cloud of dust, and the old woman pulled me over to a stump in the shade.

Rusty and the men lugged the heavy bags over and everyone ran alongside, talking excitedly now that the truck had gone. Although the Indian Affairs people are technically responsible for the health and welfare of the Pumé, they are so underfunded that they had never visited this community before, and the people were very tense at the rare appearance of governmental strangers.

The old woman, who I now know is named Rufina, sat me down on the stump while women and girls swarmed around, murmuring and giggling. Someone plumped a naked baby boy in my lap, and he squirmed while I admired his thick black hair and almond eyes with silky long lashes. A second later I nearly dropped him when he peed like a warm geyser, soaking both of us to a chorus of delighted laughter from the women.

We spent all afternoon giving away clothes and tools. Because they will be feeding us and watching out for us while we're here, in return we are giving them things they normally have a hard time trading for. Rusty was overjoyed to see his friends again; he was all smiles and jokes. He was especially goofy with a handsome young man of about 33 with a devilish goatee beard and sparkling eyes, whose name, I learned, was Pedro Julio.

Pedro Julio was voraciously curious about everything, and although I didn't understand the Pumé language, I could tell he was asking, What's that? What's that?, as he pointed to everything we unpacked. When he asked about the toilet paper, Rusty, at a loss for the right words, took a piece of it and mimed wiping his ass with a big flourish. The crowd hooted with laughter and nudged each other happily.

The Pumé dry season camp is located right on the banks of a creek so that women can fetch water from nearby wells they've dug, and also so that the men can fish nearby. The camp consists of twelve simple branch shelters, obviously intended only for shade and dry season storage, and a few tiny, conical thatched huts for dry season rain squalls. There are about 63 Pumé living in this camp. According to the latest census the total population of the Pumé tribe, scattered in communities throughout the region, is nearing 7,000, larger than many modern groups of indigenous Americans.

During the hot afternoon I sat munching on two sweet, squishy golden mangos and watched while the men set to work building a brush shelter for Rusty and me. They cleared a spot near the sparkling creek, lopped four large limbs collected from nearby trees, planted them upright, and wove in and tied a latticework of smaller branches to make a roof. Then they made a shelf for all our bags, and we put everything up out of the way of bugs, dogs, and children. I hung up our hammock and lay gratefully in it, making faces at the little girls who were constantly racing through the shelter.

The kids are anything but frightened of us. They come in herds and whisper things to me in Pumé, which I repeat back. Then they shriek with laughter and run off. I can see that they're not too skinny, but their hair is thin and damaged and the younger kids have nasty open sores on their faces. Although the adults wear clothes (mostly patchwork pants and dresses made from old clothes traded by the wealthier river Pumé), many of the kids run naked in the dry, mosquitoless season. The old men are the very last Pumé to wear the traditional loincloth that was once worn by men and women alike as their only garment.

4/15/92   All last night the Pumé danced in a ceremony they call *tohé.* It was held in a cleared dirt plaza north of the main village, with stout poles for hammocks planted in the west corner and a tall, slender pole in the circular clearing's center. In the sand, a thousand ghostly footprints swirl around the pole, which serves as the center of the circular dance. As the orange sun sank below the horizon, everyone hung up their hammock or spread mats and sat down, smoking cigars while the main singer and his wife sat alone to one side, singing softly.

Some of the men began to snort the hallucinogenic snuff, called *nanú.* It makes you drool and leak black snot out your nose, and vomit if you're not used to it. After a brief, terrifying trip you experience a long, mellow come-down. I don't think I'll be trying any soon.

The women and kids gossiped, played, or watched the men snorting nanú. After a while they clustered around my hammock, or *burí,* talking to me with lots of expressive gestures. None of the savanna Pumé speak Spanish, and I smiled uncertainly while the conversation flowed incomprehensibly around me. They were probably discussing how dumb I looked.

I didn't catch much of the dancing because I was too tired, and dozed off after midnight. At times the men stood in line, singing. The women stood to the right of them, arms around each others' waists, swaying gracefully and repeating choruses. At intervals the men would break up and run full speed around the center pole. The women joined them, staying linked at the waist in a perfect line, revolving around the pole like the hands on a clock. Very late in the night someone did a sucking cure on a sick person; all I could hear was *suck! suck! suck! Pwooo!* followed by a sobbing groan and lots of fancy belching.

The full moon, ringed by a ghostly rainbow, shone faintly down on the suspension strings of my hammock where I lay and watched, feeling like I was on Mars. I've always been disoriented and frightened in churches, and this ritual felt much more intense than any church service. By the time dawn glowed pink in the east and the dancers lined up facing the sun, I was a nervous wreck. Rusty, who had slept soundly through the whole thing, awoke fresh as a daisy and annoyingly cheerful.

4/16/92   Yesterday was spent in more language lessons, and last night just as we dropped, exhausted, into our big hammock it began to rain. From all around us in the dark came abrupt Pumé expressions of irritation as the cold drops permeated everyone's flimsy branch roofs. Rufina, the old woman who befriended me my first day, scurried into our shelter with a big woven mat and tossed it at us, muttering. Giggling, we put it over us as best we could, but our heads and feet got wet, and as the downpour got worse the moisture crept from either end of the hammock toward the middle. So my second night in Doro Aná also passed with almost no sleep.

This morning a group of Pumé came over and saw that our whole floor was soaked, with the exception of the patch directly beneath where our bodies had blocked the rain. They pointed and made impressed exclamations, and a troop of men marched off to get wood and thatch for a new house for us. Since we are in a dry season camp the branch shelters are small and impermanent, just enough to provide shade and place to hang your burí and your household goods.

Pedro Julio, the bearded young man, visited me with his two wives, Amelia and María Luisa, and Amelia's baby boy Batida (the one who soaked me the other day). Rusty tells me the Pumé have Spanish names in order to be able to talk with their *criollo*, or Spanish-Indian, neighbors, and the government uses those names for the census. I squinted and smiled while the adults talked earnestly with me, trying to get me to understand what they were saying. I haven't experienced this kind of incomprehension since I was a toddler trying to learn English. I'd forgotten what frustrating work it is.

All the food here gets shared between houses. Most of it these days is fish or mango fruit, and I like seeing the little girls, normally so rambunctious, trotting demurely from house to house with little gourd bowls of food to share with their neighbors. As I learn how to pick a fish head apart to get at the brain and the succulent fat around the eyes, I remember my father, who has always had a fondness for making the rest of our family shriek and groan when he eats fish heads. How he would enjoy this lunch!

The men hiked about one-and-a-half miles to get enough poles and thatch (from the *moriche* palm tree) to make us a real house. Five men and boys took about four hours to build it, using machetes, knives, and shovels we had brought. I was impressed at how tough they are on tools; mere metal is no match for a Pumé. Because they worked so hard, we paid them handsomely: 500 bolívares, or about $8.00 (it's tempting to give them more, but paying more than the local rate has been known to inflate local prices too quickly among other traditional groups.) My first house, paid for with my very own money! Bet this won't happen in the States for a good long while . . .

While the men worked, their womenfolk sat nearby and groomed each other. One woman will sit on the ground and another will lie gracefully down, her head in the sitting woman's lap. The groomer uses her fingers and an elegant little pointed

wood tool to kill lice and crush eggs. As I watched them, I realized I like the way they look. The Pumé are much taller and more slender than many South American groups, with skin varying from medium coffee brown to dark mahogany. As the Pumé men usually move to their wives' family's camps, the women here are all related to each other. Doro Aná women tend to have very wide cheekbones and small pointed chins. Their eyes are slanted, but only a few have really almond-shaped eyes. I wish they would stay still so I could sketch them.

4/18/92   Amazingly, it seems that the rainy season has already arrived. We've been having storms about once a day and the mosquitoes have picked up. Soon we'll have to sleep in a mosquito net, or *hii*, in the Pumé language. It's too bad; I'd begun to enjoy sleeping in our burí in the open. Although I had falling dreams when I first started sleeping suspended, I like it now. The air passes under you and cools you, and you can rock yourself to sleep. While I lie awake at night, I repeat new Pumé words over to myself in a whisper. I like how time is measured by symbols: a day is one sun, or *doh*, a month is one moon, or *gupenéh*, a season or half/year is one water, or *uí*, meaning the rainy season.

The word Pumé means people or family, and the word *niwéi* is used to describe Spanish or European-descended people, outsiders. Among themselves, the Pumé use no names, only kin terms. My name means nothing to them, and I'm having to learn to answer to *aí* (mom, as the kids call me), *amí* (big sister, as the young women call me), *keranyí* (sister-in-law, as their husbands call me), and *habí* (daughter, as the old folks call me), just for starters. It's very complicated, but it's nice to be adopted into the family.

4/21/92   Part of our data-collecting involves my following the women out on their gathering trips and writing down everything they do at the minute that it happens, and how long it takes. So far I've managed to miss every morning trip. At dawn, the women grab their baskets and digging sticks and steal quietly out of camp to gather edible plants in the cool morning hours, and I open sleep-bleared eyes just in time to see them disappearing into the misty distance.

We bathe and wash clothes in the creek nearby, but for cooking I've been hauling water from the little well dug at the edge of the creek, or *doró*. The Pumé dig wells at the edge of bodies of water so that the sand filters out most impurities, and this water is clear and cool, the cleanest and sweetest I've ever tasted. But my arms ache from the hauling.

I can't say how I feel about this project right now, let alone the discipline of anthropology. I can't believe how hard this is, how exciting, how humiliating, how confusing. I am lonely for my family. I am hungry and tired all the time. I either am constipated or have diarrhea. I want to crawl into a hole. I want to run out of here screaming. I want to do anything but stay here for another year and a half, or call anthropology my life's profession.

Rusty and a group of excited Pumé have just returned from a

fishing trip. With them was a young Pumé woman slouched half-fainting on the back of a horse. As they eased her into her house, Rusty rushed over for the medicine kit and told me that while chopping firewood the woman had dropped an axe on her foot, cutting it horribly. A criollo neighbor had kindly lent them the horse.

In the little house the woman, named Dori, lay limply in her burí, moaning with pain and fever, her pretty catlike face bathed in cold sweat. The cut on her right foot gaped deep and ugly, swollen and covered with dirt and dried blood. It was hot to the touch and looked red already. There is no hospital within a hundred miles of here, not even a tiny clinic. We were on our own.

While everyone crowded around, a few of the women weeping, we cleaned and butterfly-bandaged the wound. After giving Dori some painkillers and oral antibiotics, we walked back to our house. Rusty, tired and frightened, shed a few tears and angrily dashed them off his face, making dirty smears. "Why can't these people get even the most basic medical help?" he asked me. "Why?"

4/22/92   For once, I was ready at sunrise when I saw four old women gear up and march southward on a root-gathering trip. Rufina, Lucrecia, and the two sisters María Diachi and Diacricia (all *aí*, or mother, to me) hiked to a burned, cleared area, plumped themselves and their baskets down in the ashy sand, and dug roots in the blazing sun for the next four hours.

They dug two different kinds of roots: *pará*, which look like brown fingers covered with rough, papery bark, and *chokuí*, which are white and bulblike and covered with hairy fibers. The women squatted or sat, mining patiently for roots using a slim, square-bladed metal shovel they call a *toréh*. In times past, they used a stick flattened on one edge, but now they trade with neighboring ranchers for toréh whenever they can. Rufina, who is nearly blind, dug and sifted with her fingers to find the roots. The other women threw handfuls into her basket so she could keep up with them.

When they had enough *pará* and *chokuí* they got up and went to a shady area nearby, where they collected a fibrous root called *tuu*. On our way home, I offered to carry one of the heavy baskets and Lucrecia solemnly helped me put it on my head. The tumpline, which is the handle of the basket, goes across your forehead and the weight of the burden rests on the center of your back. Indigenous Americans and other women the world over have been using this method of carrying loads for thousands of years and it works very well. I managed to carry the basket back to camp with no spills, but I could hear stifled laughter behind me on the trail.

4/2/92 Our crude bandage job and the powerful antibiotics seem to have done the trick with Dori's foot wound. Although her husband has had to carry her out to the bushes to pee for a few days, she's beginning to heal and will be walking soon, we hope.

My "mother" Rufina lives with her son and his family in the shelter next door. She comes over often and shows me the various roots I need to know about, including pará, chokuí, and a wrinkly, dried buttonlike root called *yipái* that isn't in season yet. She also comes over and shares her food with us.

Rufina's son, Francisco, is Rusty's age, and since he's the only Pumé here who understands and speaks a little Spanish, he's the *capitán*, or village spokesman, in dealings with Spanish neighbors and officials. Yesterday, Francisco brought in a big load of fish, the toothy kind called *dapué*. Rufina quickly fanned up the fire and cut the fish into the pot, adding water and a little precious salt. She fanned the stew to a boil, then turned to yell at one of her granddaughters. The pot was propped precariously on three rocks, and as she turned back she bumped it and the whole potful of boiling fish spilled out onto the sand.

Muttering angrily, the old woman scooped the muddy fish up with her hands and slapped them back into the pot. Biting our cheeks, Rusty and I kept from laughing, but when little Olga came over with a bowl of fish mud stew to share with us, I told the little girl untruthfully that we weren't hungry.

4/24/92   Yesterday, very early, I ran out after a bunch of women and boys to go mango-gathering. We walked about twelve kilometers, or about six miles, in the blazing sun, and I finished my canteen of water in the first hour. Along the way a young man named Juan Masano spotted an armadillo digging busily by the side of the trail. I watched, amazed, as he walked casually up to the armadillo's rear end, which was sticking out of the hole, and pulled it out by the tail. He stepped on its neck, then jerked sharply up on the tail to break the spine.

I had expected wild animals to be a little harder to kill! Juan walked up to me and handed me the dead armadillo. Being a male, it had an erection (they have bizarre, three-pronged penises) and its pink tongue was protruding from its tiny snout. I hurriedly stuffed it head first into my sidepack and jogged to catch up with the others.

We picked mangos at the ranch of a wealthy man, renowned for his big grove of mango trees and for his unscrupulous attempts to force the Pumé off their land. Luckily, we didn't run into him, only his wife, who was kind enough to give me a cup of coffee, black and stickily sweet to my parched mouth. Hours later, loaded down with up to eighty pounds of mango apiece, the Pumé started off for home. The fierce sun took its toll, and by the end of the trip Amelia was whimpering with exhaustion. One of the older men took some of her load, which had been about sixty pounds. I myself had only a few mangos and the armadillo in my little pack, but nearly dropped in my tracks from the heat and the long hike.

4/27/92 The day before yesterday I saw Rufina wander off with a taiyó basket and a machete in the early morning. She returned an hour later with a basketful of small fish for the pot. Rusty has seen the women wade into shallow ponds and whack the water with machetes to stun small fish, and I think this is how Rufina got her catch today. As I've also seen the men gather yipái on their fishing trips, it seems that the boundaries occasionally blur in the Pumé system of sexual division of labor.

Yesterday two old men, Trino and his brother-in-law Dos Pasos, went to the pond where Trino's wife Lucrecia had left a basketful of pará roots to soak during our trip five days ago. The men brought back the roots and dumped them into a big hole lined with leaves. They then added more leaves (from a plant called *mishotóh*) and pounded the smelly mixture into a dark, smelly sludge. The Pumé use several different fish poisons, and this kind is new to us. All the poisons work by blocking the fish's oxygen intake, so that the fish suffocate and float to the surface. Amazingly, the fish are not only safe to eat, but they taste good, too.

I find myself wondering whether we brought enough medical supplies. Last night Teresa, Dionso's little daughter, was playing toss-the-knife with her obnoxious older brother, José. José wound up and really got her in the upper thigh. When we arrived, we could see that her leg was laid open for about six inches, the pink muscles twitching like snakes in the beam of our flashlight. While she lay in her father's lap, we bathed and closed the gaping wound with butterfly bandages, the same as we had with Dori's foot wound. The little girl was asleep from boredom well before we'd finished. They make Pumé kids pretty tough.

4/29/92   Rusty is now trying to teach me the fine points of how to take data. We have four main jobs: walking around the village at hourly intervals and writing down what people are doing; sitting in people's houses for four-hour periods to record a continuous stream of activities; recording particular manufacturing events like arrow-making or weaving; and following the Pumé out on hunting and gathering trips. Today I tried my first "focal household," without much success. I felt incredibly nosy and obtrusive, sitting in a house and writing every time someone in the family scratched themselves, and after only two hours I got up and slinked away to the vast relief of all.

Part of the problem is that I feel the power and direction of gaze here more than I ever have before—it's like my skin is gone when these people look at me. It doesn't help that the houses have no walls and are about three feet apart. Conversely, I feel that the Pumé are able to tell I'm looking at them even when their backs are turned. Is this just our first painful shyness with each other, or will it be like this the whole time?

There are more girls than boys in this camp, and I've been startled by the intensity of their play. I'm used to the stereotype of girls playing house and boys playing football, but here, as at home, children's behavior confounds adult expectations. Young Pumé girls have excellent hand-eye coordination and throw rocks or slimy mango pits with deadly accuracy. In addition to playing house, they do more high-speed running, climbing, swimming, and wrestling than any of the boys I remember from my childhood.

María Florenzia next door is dishing out fish to share with everyone, and I ponder how generosity operates here. The two most influential houses in Doro Aná are hers (she is Francisco's wife) and Lucrecia's (Trino's wife). Francisco is capitán of the village, and Trino was before him, and their families always share out whatever food they have, holding back only enough to feed themselves.

On the other hand, the lowest man on the totem pole here, Dionso, is so stingy that his own children go begging to other people's houses, having been denied food at home. Needless to say, he and his wife hoard food and goods, never share with other families, and are barely tolerated in the community. In other words, the capitalist ideal of self-profit is a secret shame to the person who practices it here, and an embarrassment to his neighbors and family.

4/30/92   I felt antsy today and decided to take a walk by myself. I wandered over to the empty wet season camp, about one-half mile to the south, near to the burned area where I went with the old women to gather roots a week ago. I sniffed around the big, solidly thatched houses, some of which can shelter several families from the torrential rains of winter.

I was impressed by how brittle the trash was in the household trash heaps, sun-baked and rain-soaked daily. There wouldn't be much left to find in a hundred years; no wonder there are so few archaeological sites found in this area. The Pumé have never had access to any workable form of stone, and before metal arrived here they always relied on plant and animal parts for their technology. This caused me to realize for the first time how underrepresented plant materials, the main focus of female technology across the world, must be in any archaeological site.

When I got back home, old Lucrecia came running up, scolding me and asking where I'd run off to. Although I couldn't understand everything she said, she rubbed her eyes in a pantomime of crying and I got the idea she'd really been worried about me. I felt guilty for scaring them like that; they still don't trust me to wander around without getting lost.

Today Dori, whose injured foot is still healing, came limping over to our house with two big hunks of fish, one for Rusty and one for me. I wasn't there, so Dori handed Rusty the fish, saying, "Give the bigger piece with eggs in it to your wife." I was tickled, first because it was kind of her and second because she assumed Rusty really *would* give me the bigger piece. Which he did, of course.

As I write, the sound of Francisco sneezing next door floats over to us. The Pumé love to sneeze, and adults and children will poke a piece of grass or a twig up one nostril, bringing on fits that will last for minutes. Their faces look oddly calm, almost entranced as they explode with sneeze after sneeze.

5/3/92   Today Rusty went on a hunting trip and returned with a little present for me. The men had come across a rotten palm stump full of *kuyú*, or palm beetle larvae. They'd eaten them right then and there, but Rusty stashed one for me because I'd never had one before. He proudly fished it out of his bag and handed it

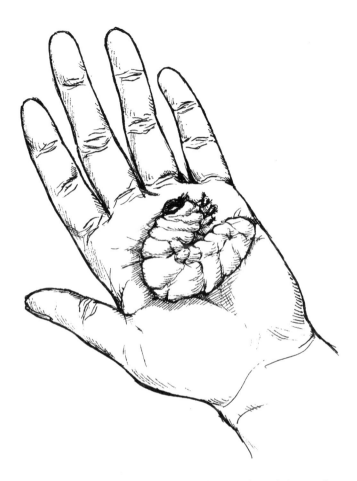

to me. It was larger than my thumb, white, soft and fat, with a bristly black head and angrily biting jaws. It writhed slowly in my hand as I stared at it uncertainly. "Do you . . . just . . . eat it raw?" I asked. "Bite off the head first, or it'll nip your tongue," Rusty advised.

Deciding not to think about it any longer, I gingerly bit off the snapping head and spat it out, then quickly shoved the struggling body into my mouth and chewed, my eyes closed. It was creamy, with a vague sweet spicy taste like eggnog. "Have you got any more of those?" I asked hopefully.

5/5/92   Since it's a delicate matter for Rusty to ask for women's personal items in trade, he obtained very few of them on his last trip here. This morning we noticed some *go-aburé*, or women's loincloths (equivalent to panties), drying on Lucrecia's roof.

I walked over with a spool of thread and tried to tell her, with sign language and a few words of Pumé, that I wanted to trade for one of her loincloths. Lucrecia shrugged and took one off of the roof and handed it to me. I then asked her how to put it on. Lucrecia looked down at her pretty little granddaughter, Newe, who was watching curiously, and they both giggled. I hid behind a tree, looked around, and dropped my pants. Lucrecia, still smiling, showed me how to take the beautiful dyed red palm fibers and tuck them into a twisted cotton string belt she tied around my waist. The go-aburé was the only Pumé female garment before cloth dresses became available thirty years ago. I think the Pumé adopted dresses very rapidly, mostly in order to keep a layer of cloth between them and the biting insects of the upcoming wet season.

5/6/92   I sometimes wonder if the Pumé ever get depressed; mostly they seem too busy to bother with it. Right now with everyone gone out visiting we have no data to write down and I'm feeling miserable. I miss my friends and I chipped a molar on a rock in yesterday's fish breakfast.

Little Newe is hanging around with me, watching me write. I think she's as restless as I am today. I look down at her little smiling face covered with mango juice and wonder if she'll be living this way as a grown-up woman Pumé. Or will she be like one of those Indian elders in North America in the 1920s, whose every reminiscence was sifted through by ethnologists and folklorists, whose smallest memory was more precious and unique than the most flawless diamond? Will Newe's grandchildren be informants, whom oral historians will mine for tiny, exhausted veins of third-hand knowledge about the Pumé way of life?

If this area is made into a national park (as the Venezuelan Park Service would like to do), where will the Pumé, as undesirable human squatters, be able to go? Will they become tenant ranchers, lose their language and traditions and become thinner, browner criollos? Or will they be relocated by the government to hellish, booze-soaked hamlets like Chenchenita? Will they be allowed to stay only under the condition that they remain "picturesque," turning down modern medicines, tools, and rifles while they watch their children go hungry? All of these things have happened with hunter-gatherers in Alaska, Peru, and Africa, when their land was in demand, whether from the ranchers, the farmers, the oil companies, or eco-tourism. What could Rusty and I do to help?

The distance between our two worlds is immense, and I, with one foot in each, can feel myself doing the splits. When I think of all the surplus it takes to make a can of Coke, I am overwhelmed. How on earth did we get from here to there? Newe is singing softly to herself as she watches me write. My mind is going numb with unanswered questions.

5/7/92   The wind is blowing this morning, very cool and sweet. I am extremely hungry. Is this wind better than an artichoke with vinegar dressing? Better than a big bowl of pasta with cheese sauce? Better than a candy bar? The odors of rain and unknown grasses, of distant, dew-soaked morning earth blow into my little open-ended house. My belly is empty and my mouth is dry, but this wind feeds my nose and my skin with all the perfumed richness of the llanos.

Pedro Julio, his father Trino, and Rusty are building us a brand-new, well-thatched house a half mile away up the hill, in the wet season camp. I am running tobacco and water to the men, who have done seven hours' hard labor in the scorching heat with nothing to eat since yesterday afternoon. Water and a couple of cigars are all they have to keep them going. On the way up, P.J. showed me a large snake he'd killed earlier with a shovel. It was beautiful, deep golden with chocolate stripes and a creamy white belly, and it had no fangs. But the Pumé kill all snakes anywhere near camp; they've had enough encounters with venomous ones and they take no chances.

5/9/92   When I get back to the States I'm going to try to market a few earth-friendly, politically correct Pumé household helpers. These might include:

> *Pumé All-Purpose Seasoning:*
> 1 part salt, 1 part charred wood fragments, 8 parts dirt. Best for fish and meats. About one handful per pot recommended.

> *Pumé Dishwashing Detergent:*
> Sandy dirt. For those tough jobs, add small rocks.

> *Pumé Bandaids:*
> For small cuts, rub dirt well in, then bind tightly with a rag, preferably dirty. (Why ruin a new piece of cloth by getting blood on it?)

5/10/92   Impressions of another night dance: Little Manisanta, who is still nursing, sits in her mother's lap. The three-year-old takes turns sucking at her mother's breast and puffing on a home-made cigar. The women hold each other around the waist while standing or dancing. They trot with bare feet in perfect step around the pole, singing, never missing a beat. When babies or young children cry for their parents, the mother or father will leave the plaza, pick up the child, and return to the dance still holding the child to the breast or on the shoulders (the thud of your parents' dancing feet beneath you, the vibration of their singing voices in their chests and throats!).

Just before dawn the fireflies, which had been flashing sporadically, suddenly synchronized. Hundreds of them exploded with light at the same instant, about every seven seconds, until dawn. The effect, as the insects surrounded the plaza and were interspersed with the dancers, was spectacular and eerie.

Yesterday Dori secretly offered me some sweet, squishy ripe mangos. She made sure I wiped the dirt off them before I ate them, and later even whispered her name to me, which is a very rare thing for the Pumé to do. I noted with pleasure that her foot is nearly as good as new, with a nice plum-colored scar like a crescent moon.

Dori has a beautiful triangular face with enormous slanted brown eyes over very sharp cheekbones. Her chin is pointed and fragile, her nose and mouth small and kittenish. She has no children but takes care of her husband's son by a former wife, and she is old enough to have a matronly wrinkle to her brow and a purse to her lips. She wears her hair in a little braid, usually tied with a bit of cloth ribbon. She calls me big sister, or amí.

The Pumé in Their Wet Season Camp

5/12/92   Nearly everyone has packed up and moved to the wet season camp. Our house up there is still unfinished and Francisco's family is staying behind with us until it's done.

The savanna lies under silvery gray skies with dewdrops on every blade of white-haired grass. The air is alive with insects new-hatched and the birds are leaving, flying north. The way the trees writhe up out of the mist with their sparse tops gives them the illusion of being about to topple over with the slightest breeze. Actually, their wood is really hard; the sound of a chopping axe rings clear and musical even at a distance.

I have found a group of sensuous magenta orchids growing in the mossy crotch of a tree by our bathing pond. The whole world is waking up to the rains, plants bursting into flower and leaf overnight. I hope we can move before we're flooded out.

5/14/92   Early this morning, with dark purple clouds glowering overhead, we packed up and a group of Pumé men helped us lug everything up to the wet season camp. Our lovely new house is very high and wide, with a clean, hard-packed sandy floor unlike the black dust in the dry season camp. It stormed right away, but the small leaks in the roof actually stopped after a few minutes! We guess it's because the thatch swells with the moisture and seals off small cracks. I like this house already.

Since the water level has yet to rise high enough to be near to camp, women and girls have to walk about a quarter-mile every time we need water. The babies are always left behind in camp with the old women or younger girls. Of course, the babies throw spectacular fits when their mothers leave them and are inconsolable for about five minutes. One little girl of about two, named Domana, will run after her mother, stop at the edge of camp, and howl angrily after her mother's receding silhouette.

I remember how desolate I used to feel when Mom used to leave for work. I had always had this cherished notion that mothers in a more traditional setting spend more time with their children than modern working mothers in industrialized countries. In reality, I've seen Pumé babies farmed out regularly to other households if the mother is going somewhere, or even if she's just busy or needs a break. So maybe another of our stereotypes, that of the "normal" mother secluded at home with the kids all day long, shows an exception rather than the rule in human family life.

5/16/92   I'm feeling more and more at home recording data. This morning I went fishing with Gonzalo and his young wife Gusha, who helped her husband by digging worms and gutting fish. This is harder work than it sounds. The rain misted down on us the whole time and we got home soaked and muddy.

It strikes me every time I approach camp how the first sound that always floats out to me is laughter. These people, so hungry and poor, surrounded by incomprehensible dangers in all directions, laugh and sing all day long.

5/18/92   Last night I danced at tohé for the first time. I stood between my two favorite old women, Rufina and Lucrecia, and swayed enthusiastically. Although we certainly didn't embody the Three Graces, I think people appreciated the effort. Somehow I kept bumping butts with the old women, and stifled snorts of laughter erupted out of the darkness around us while Lucrecia and Rufina struggled to maintain their dignity.

5/19/92   As we get hungrier and hungrier with the onset of the wet season, I find that food is central to my thoughts. My relationship with Rusty, so absorbing to me before, now takes a backseat to whether we are fed or not. I haven't yet deteriorated to where I'd steal food, and, of course, it's nearly impossible to deny food to begging children in the house.

Still, I find myself monitoring my own body and its needs intently. I cram food into my mouth as quickly as I can and snarl at waiting dogs. I peer under the eaves to see what's cooking next door. When I see women walking toward our house with food to share, I get a surge of happiness like I haven't felt since I was a baby. In the States, food is my enemy, seductive and fattening. Here, food is security; all comfort, health, and happiness is a full belly.

5/21/92   The Pumé women are astonishingly versatile in their approaches to me, depending on what they're after. They are very sly when negotiating a trade with me, and proper and matronly when telling me my floor needs sweeping or my boiling mangos are ready to take off the fire. But they giggle like children when I try to dance at tohé or otherwise make a spectacle of myself, and when they are sick or hurt and need medicine they are truly pathetic, with high, weak voices, trembling mouths, and eyes brimming with tears.

5/22/92   An intense tohé: This night we cling like limpets to the barren rock of the night while the backward-rushing tide of time leaves us to die under the merciless sun. We hang on like suckerfish to the earth's leathery hide as she swims in a circle. We face east all night, driving the planet like a car through the dark hours, singing and talking to keep each other company, keep each other awake. I can feel the seeds of my own death ripening within me, and I accept it. Pedro Julio sings in a high, cracked voice in the predawn blackness—possessed by a she-spirit! I can't see his face, I don't even recognize his voice; I can feel the hairs stand up on the back of my neck.

This morning I am exhausted. Through drooping eyelids I watch Docha María, Eulogio's elder daughter, as she sits companionably with little Chita on a mound of dirt in the rain. Both are cheerful as robins and naked as the dawn.

Before I fade off into a morning nap I giggle to remember Pedro Julio last night, before the dance started, cutting a series of noisy, pungent farts. Amid the appreciative laughter of nearby men, he named each fart as he let it rip: "Here comes the Giant Anteater Toenail! And the Big Fish Head! And old Grampa!"

5/30/92   We've spent the last few days mapping the dry season village, where we spent our first month. These maps will be interesting to compare to maps of prehistoric North American Indian and other hunter-gatherer sites around the world. Yesterday we paid a visit to the nearest ranch, about four miles to the north. It's owned by old Don Armando Aguilar, who sat and ate a terrific lunch with us; real criollo cooking, rich and spicy. Don Armando has great fondness for the Pumé; he is an old friend of Trino's, and pays the Pumé reasonably for work they sometimes do on the ranch. It's nice to get to know our neighbors a little better.

6/3/92   I went on a mango gathering trip this morning with my "father" Trino and his two wives, Lucrecia and Diacricia. When we got to the grove of trees, Trino cut and trimmed a stick to hook the fruit with, and climbed nimbly up a tree. While he knocked the fruit down, the old women scrambled to pick it up, tossing each piece into taiyó baskets. The two wives harangued their husband while he squinted around in the leafy branches; he's hard of hearing and the women had to shout and whack the tree trunk to draw his attention to ripe mangos he was missing. I laughed heartily at this example of conjugal cooperation, while the women yelled in high exasperated voices, "Hey! The ripe ones are over there! OVER THERE! Hey!" I think Trino sometimes pretends to be more deaf than he really is.

Back home with the mangos, Lucrecia sends her granddaughter Newe out for water. As I watch the little girl struggle with the heavy bucket, I think about her situation. An epidemic of measles in 1986 raged out of control, and many Pumé died throughout the llanos. Newe lost both her parents to the plague and is being brought up by Trino and Lucrecia, her mother's parents. Her cousin, Manewi, lost her mother to the measles and her father to another wife. So she lives with her own grandmother Diacricia in the same house, and the two girls are like sisters.

Newe, about six years old, is a favorite of mine. She is built like a little fawn, very slender with a long gentle face and big eyes like her grandmother. Her little chin is pointed, her hair wispy and flyaway. Her skin is very light coffee and cream, unlike the other Pumé children. Being an orphan, she works extra hard, carrying water and tending babies. But between jobs she manages to run and play with the other girls, and always has a big bright smile for me. When hurt or angry she is a real tragedy queen, hurling herself on her belly in the dirt and weeping musically. But if no one pays attention she heaves herself up and walks unsteadily home, rubbing her eyes and sniffling as if she were on her way to fling herself off a cliff in the moonlight.

Her polar opposite is her cousin and playmate Manisanta, about four years old. She is very dark with pink palms and foot-soles; her joints are already big and her limbs brawny and well muscled. She walks with a swagger, like a cowboy on her way to a showdown. Manisanta loves puppies, and will haul them around by their hindlegs while they whimper piteously. She will crush them to her chest, pound them with her fist, and cover them with kisses in the space of ten seconds. She climbs and swims better than any other kid in camp, and is a deadly shot with rocks. Of course, she is a constant presence in our house, with goopy mango-hands or fish-hands that need to grab everything.

6/5/92   Wet season nights are the hardest. I lie sweltering inside the *hii*, or mosquito net, with Rusty's sweaty side pressed against mine and millions of mosquitoes singing evilly outside the net-

ting. When I tap the netting with my finger, their song gets high-pitched and agitated as they take to the air. I have scratched my bites so much that my skin is bruised and scabbed; I often find myself scratching in my sleep.

I have swollen glands, a sore throat, fever with hallucinations, and almost no sleep for days. Everybody else has colds, too; the aspirin we brought are being chomped down like candy. The morning air is permeated by the thin wails of babies and wet, wretched coughs. I guess people are getting weaker from the lack of food—the fish have dispersed into the growing flooded areas, game is scarce, and the wild roots and garden crops still haven't swelled enough from the rains to be edible. Everyone is surviving on bitter green mangos and tiny, button-sized roots.

Today, while some Pumé were socializing with us in our house, Encarnación, a nosy teenager, was rooting through one of our baskets hanging in the roof. He surfaced with my bag of tampons. "What are these?" he asked innocently. I looked at Rusty, who explained matter-of-factly, "Those are for menstrual blood. They go in the vagina." Wow! Everyone hooted with unbelieving laughter as the bag was passed around for inspection. What will those crazy niwéi think of next?

6/7/92   Along with a refreshing rain storm comes a blessed spate of letters from home, quenching my parched sense of self and riveting me for hours. The letters were forwarded by the Indian Affairs office and took several months to reach us.

They remind me how differently time flows for us here. In Doro Aná we tell over the brightly colored beads of our unnamed days as they come: this is a hot day, this a buggy day, this a sleepy day, this a fish catch day, a mango picking day. Outside, the troubled, crowded world wobbles on its axis; there are fires, riots, elections, nations rise and fall . . . but here I sit listening to the mosquitoes whining, the children singing, and the birds talking in the mango trees. All peace and happiness on earth would come to a point in this little village if I had a big plate of food in my lap and well-fed Pumé all around me.

Right now, Rusty is playing *tikirí* with Micheda, Teresa and José outside our house. The tikirí, which resemble tiny tops, are among a number of ingenious toys the children invent out of trash and household odds and ends. You flip one, spinning, onto the sand while your opponent flips his or her tikirí at yours and tries to hit it, ruining its spin. You keep every one you hit. Looking under the eaves, I can see Rusty's big booted feet, the children's small brown feet, and the tikirí spinning, as the players shout excitedly.

6/9/92   This morning I went on a gathering trip with a group of hungry young women and girls. We didn't get much, just a few *tochó* pods from trees near the creek. Both the tough peel and the soft inner skin are removed from the seed, which can be eaten raw. If you can control your munching long enough to get a few of them home, tochó seeds roasted or boiled taste like bitter lima beans.

Not much return, I thought, for a couple hours' gathering. I contrast the Pumé food resource base to that of Oregon's Klamath Indians, with whom I am familiar. The foods available to the Klamath during most of the year would boggle a Pumé's mind. The lake-lily seeds, harvested by the ton, the huckleberries, the cattail roots, the salmon, elk, waterfowl, and deer! I wonder, before the Spanish arrived in this part of Venezuela, did the Pumé have a larger choice of foods? Could the hunger here, which is so severe, be something new, caused by the ever-shrinking Pumé land base? The Klamath used to chew the inner bark of the ponderosa pine during starvation time, in the early spring. For the Pumé, starvation time is year-round.

As the hunger intensifies, we're being flooded with requests that we go to the ranch and buy rice. Unfortunately, we have only enough money to buy food at intervals we've already set, and we can't afford extra purchases. Besides, if we bought them food now it would only last a day or two and the Pumé would then be thrown back on their own resources. No food stamps in the llanos. It's for this reason we've decided to eat the way they do, or more accurately, to go without.

I've explained the best I can to the old women why we can't buy food now. It probably didn't make them any less hungry, but I want them to know we're doing the best we can with our limited money. Still, if it gets to the point where nursing mothers start to run out of milk for their babies, I might have to do something drastic like send to the States for more money. Non-interference is very well on paper, and we'll stick to it as long as we can, but no babies will die of starvation in Doro Aná while we're here.

6/11/92   The wet season creeps by. I play with little crippled Chita, help blind Rufina gather roots, medicate horrible running sores on the children's heads and arms, and take the time to give a caress to a dying puppy who is blindly seeking the warmth of our hearth. It's probably the first and the last such touch he'll ever feel, but I, who will go on living, feel better for it.

6/15/92   With some of the beads we gave the Pumé last month they went to another village and traded for a pig. Other Pumé, with more access to processed foods like rice, sometimes manage to raise a pig or two. We lost no time in killing and eating it; pigs don't last very long in Doro Aná. The feel of a full belly!

It's pretty common for us to eat a fair number of gnats and mosquitoes along with our food. The bugs concentrate so densely around us they fly in our mouths, eyes, and noses, they get stuck in food, they drown in drink. As for bites, I'm covered head to toe; I've never been so aware of my body as a landscape to be crawled on, swarmed around, lit upon, colonized, and sucked on.

The other day while I sat, freshly bathed, and tried to chit-chat with some women, Lucrecia braided up my hair while it was still wet. She commented on how thick it was and compared me to Gusha, whose glorious black hair I've always admired. Then Lucrecia lowered her voice: "You really ought to braid your hair more often. That way it won't get tangled in the burí strings when you two are fooling around at night!" The women sitting nearby rolled their eyes and giggled while I blushed furiously.

Yesterday we had our first big batch of *tambái* cakes, or *cassava*, as the Spanish call them. The bitter manioc roots, called *bai* in Pumé, are grown in small gardens. Because the soil is so poor, these roots are one of the only crops the Pumé are able to cultivate with any success.

After they're harvested, the roots are peeled, then grated using old motor-oil cans that are flattened and have nail holes punched in them. The grated root is wrung dry of all its liquid, which contains a form of cyanide. The liquid is set aside to be boiled later, and the wrung lumps are broken up and sifted into flour. This flour is sprinkled over the bottom of a hot cauldron and flipped using the belly plate of a small turtle.

When the women pull the hot cakes expertly off the fire with their fingers, they toss them onto the *tabadá* mats, where the cakes make the loveliest steamy "Whump!": Although they are pure carbohydrate and have almost no nutritional content, they sure taste good on an empty belly—starchy sweet, spongy, slightly sticky. I watched Newe cross the plaza with a fresh tambái to share out; she took the cake and pressed its fragrant, moist warmth to her face, eyes blissfully closed. All the scents of home, comfort, and motherhood combine in a fresh, softly steaming tambái.

6/21/92   Today while looking over young Chita's head for sores to treat, I caressed her little face with both hands and was surprised by the silken warmth of her cheek. I've handled many children but never in my life have I felt anything as smooth as Chita's skin.

6/25/92   This morning P.J. came over with a big grin and a basketful of manioc roots. Since his wife Amelia had already peeled them for me, I borrowed a grater from Lucrecia and, surrounded by amused Pumé, I started to grate the big, slippery roots, awkwardly scraping my fingertips. I learned the special Pumé wringing technique from Amelia, and afterward sifted the lumps into flour.

P.J. helped me cook the cakes, which came out stiff, but tasty. I boiled the liquid left over from the wringing, and after more than an hour we had a cupful apiece of hot, piercingly sweet, brown *bai uí*, or "manioc water," from which all the toxins had been boiled off.

While I walked proudly around from house to house sharing out my little tambái, Francisco showed me a beautiful male tortoise he'd caught out hunting. It was about two feet long and heavy, with a brightly patterned shell waisted like an hourglass, and brilliant red spots on its legs. He offered me one of those colorful legs and I boiled it up at home. The tambái were delicious dipped in the broth.

The llanos is fully flooded now, with still pools of water stretching for acres and gazing up at the soft silvery gray sky, punctuated by millions of waving green shoots. The dry season camp where we stayed in April is now waist-deep in water, and new-hatched baby fish swim in and out of the housepoles and float over old hearths. The soil is soft black pudding, hard to walk through, and on the hard-packed wet sand of the dunes you can see the tracks of deer, lizards, foxes, and armadillos like hieroglyphs. And the bugs dance and sing and drink our blood joyously; it's their time and they seem to know it.

6/30/92   Rusty is back from a hunting and trading trip with P.J. and a few other men, and I am amused at his guilty inventory of the field snacks they've shared among themselves (one duck egg, one armadillo, one small lizard, and a few small pieces of beef). I've rarely seen women snack on *their* gathering trips. I wonder why men snack and women don't, and whether it makes a difference in overall nutrition.

Maybe it's partly because men's foods (fish and game) can be roasted quickly and easily away from home, but women's roots often require boiling or roasting for hours. Who wants to lug a pot that far, let alone be away from your kids for that long? But since women have all the demands of menstruation, pregnancy, and lactation I can scarcely believe that they don't notice men copping protein by snacking in the field instead of bringing all of their catches home. There must be something I'm missing in this picture—I *do* know that the women control all the preparation and distribution of food once it gets to the house. Maybe they "make up" for the inequality then.

This afternoon, while I was carefully picking apart the vertebrae of a baby armadillo in order to suck out the creamy white spinal cord, I realized that I'm getting used to living here. A little familiarity is a vast comfort.

7/6/92   Today the sun is shining and the wind is blowing and the gnats are biting and the kids are playing in a mango tree and thunder rumbles distantly in the east. Camp is haunted by tiny scarlet birds with black wings, which sit fatly on the bushes like beads of blood or flash through the air after insects.

This morning at dawn we heard a repeating two-note piping hoot, a pause, and then a series of lower hoots. A queer primordial cry, an achaeopteryx song. P.J. tells us it's one of the animals closely related to the Pumé, a spirit bird. Things like this spooky cry, or the roaring of howler monkeys down by the river, a baby jaguar treed by the dogs outside of camp, or a terrible burn on Rusty's hand from a plant alkaloid, remind me anew how far away we are from home.

7/8/92   Last night I decided to go to tohé, which I'd been avoiding. The weather obliged by being still and humid and perfect for the insects to emerge and bite mercilessly.

While I sat and swatted and listened to the singing, I remembered it was my birthday. I was visited by memories of all the suppers I helped my mother cook when I was little. I remembered particularly cutting up cheese or hot dogs, because they were easy, and putting cream cheese on celery sticks I'd proudly topped and split myself. Suddenly I jumped up and ran out to the dark grove of mangos, and burst into tears. I was overwhelmed by my earliest memories of my mother as a big, warm, soft, salty-smelling presence who would hold me, sing and talk, feed me bits of peeled apple. When Rusty came out to find me, he asked what was wrong. "*I want my mother!*" I bawled like a three-year-old.

The Pumé Tough Out the Wet Season

In which we sample the ranchers' hospitality;

a wild crossing; cannibalistic musings; an owl spirit;

a robbery foiled; we snatch a baby from the jaws of

death; we bring the lightning down; crocodile stew;

Francisco and María Florenzia; Eulogio and

Docharanyí; Amelia; we all get skinnier;

chokuí from heaven

7/9/92   For my birthday present, we're going to stay a couple of days at Don Armando's ranch to rest and eat. This morning, as we slogged through the pastures and I noticed noisy sandpiper-like birds screaming at us, I had to laugh. When I first got here, I was full of well-fed, well-educated curiosity about each new animal I saw; I wanted to know their names, feeding, and mating habits, and so on. Three months later I glance at whatever it is and wonder (1) if it's good to eat, and (2) if it's hard to catch.

7/10/92   Well, after two days of ranch hospitality our bellies are temporarily taut with delicious spicy criollo cooking. This morning a group of Pumé men, women, and boys came hiking over to pick us up and to make sure we were buying them some rice and noodles at the ranch's little store, the only one for miles around. We bought food, loaded up, and marched out under the darkening clouds. If you look up "frustration" in the llanos dictionary, you'll find the entry: "Hiking into a huge thunderstorm with a heavy load on your back and the smell of garlic simmering in oil behind you."

When the first group of us, already drenched with rain, reached the flooded creek, some of the men hauled a light raft made of palm stems out from behind some bushes where it had been stored. We loaded the precious food onto it and the teenager Genaro gracefully poled it across. The rest of us had to wade for it. I ventured into the powerful current, about five and a half feet deep, and suddenly felt hands grabbing me around both arms, my neck, and my waist. Amelia, María Llovina, María Diachi, and young Luis Mende, all shorter and lighter than me, had decided that I looked like a good bet to make it across.

Loaded down like a Christmas tree, I struggled through the current. There were lots of hidden roots and rocks underfoot, and I had to use all my coordination to keep from falling or stomping on the toes of my passengers when one or more of us slipped, which was every few steps. I whooped through the whole ordeal and even considered asking the shivering Pumé to go back across with me again, but good sense and the pouring rain prevailed.

We gave away the food and some gifts of clothes and tools we'd kept stored at the ranch, and after the usual pandemonium ("Hey! My daughter didn't get any of those! Hey! You forgot Uncle again!"), we tried to wring the water out of our clothes and set our little house back in order.

7/15/92   All the men, including Rusty, are out of camp in search of game. Between hourly scans of the houses, I sit enjoying the slanting milky sunlight and cool wind. The clouds are gray and box-shaped, and they amble across the horizon like Don Armando's pretty Brahma cows grazing along a fenceline.

The shaggy thatch on my house is tawny gold in the shade and silver in the sun. Docharanyí is a shadow sitting on her floor across the plaza, wringing grated bai roots with endless graceful gyrations of her strong arms. There are five fat quail foraging in a nearby garden. Young Micheda is singing hoarsely to her baby brother José Ahi, who is crying obstinately next door. The wind is blowing the gnats around and the little blood-red bird sits in a nearby mango tree shivering, ready to pounce. He's pounced. This has got to be the longest morning in the history of the Earth; next to it the Precambrian Era looks like an eye-blink.

7/16/92   Last night as I lay in the burí, belly growling, I found myself wondering sleepily how good human flesh would taste. Abruptly I realized I was *seriously* wondering about it. I guess that's the acid test of hunger . . .

7/22/92   All day the rain permeated the air, hanging like an unanswered question. Last night there was no dance, and everyone was nearly asleep in the warm, moist darkness when an enormous owl began to hoot in the distance. The throaty, echoing calls woke everyone up, and P.J. called to the owl as the spirit of a long-dead ancestor, telling it the Pumé had no tobacco to offer (spirits love a good smoke). The owl interspersed P.J.'s long speech with hoots, and it really did sound eerily like a conversation.

7/25/92   Today Pancho Mena, who is P.J.'s older brother and lives in another village, came over with his wife Juana Trina and their three daughters. The reason they came was obvious: the baby girl was very sick and her parents wanted P.J., a famous healer, to do a cure. They began tohé early, and P.J. went through his repertoire including singing, chanting, sucking on the baby's torso, and spitting water on her belly.

The baby was wizened-looking with sunken eyes and thin, limp arms and legs. She meowed weakly through the whole procedure and jerked around rhythmically like a wind-up toy. Her eyes were fixed and unseeing, and she couldn't suck at her mother's breast. P.J.'s opening song was very gentle and lilting, like a lullaby for his suffering niece.

I don't know the baby or her parents, and instead of feeling worry or grief I feel only horror, frustration, and pity, the abstract kind you get when reading about dying babies in the newspaper. This morning the family returned to their village, the baby girl clinging stubbornly to life with tiny finger- and toenails. In desperation, we have given them a mild antibiotic for her, along with oral instructions.

7/30/92   Many rainy days leak slowly into each other. Beautiful fresh-molted butterflies of silver and black, orange and black, orange and gray, and red and black haunt the tall grasses, floating like benevolent afterthoughts through dense clouds of gnats and mosquitoes. This morning in the rising sun I could see millions of spider webs upturned like little gossamer bowls in the dew-sparkling grass. In the center of each web sat a fat brown spider, its abdomen furred with silver dewdrops.

This afternoon the men snorted nanú in our house before a dance. As they sat hunched over, sneezing and retching, tears and black mucus dripping down into their mouths, P.J. leaned over to Rusty, proffering the paddle and snorter. Smiling broadly, he said with deep relish, "*Há wu!*" or "Go for it!" like he was offering a best friend the most sumptuous of delicacies. Rusty, who only does the drug rarely and out of social obligation, reared back and refused. The expression on his face, of mingled revulsion and nausea thinly masked with politeness, was so funny I had to bite my cheeks to keep from laughing.

8/1/92   I've just found out how shameful robbery is to the savanna Pumé. Last night while I was lying in the burí by myself (Rusty was at dance), I heard someone in the house, slowly unzipping a bag. Thinking it was Rusty, I asked, "Hey, what's up?" I heard the sound of bare feet walking quickly out. When Rusty did show up I told him about it and he checked the bag. Nothing was missing, but he told me he'd found money missing earlier in the month.

When he told Francisco about it everyone came running over, excited and scandalized. Francisco orated loudly, saying that we are generous and no one should steal from us. He added that when the Pumé steal, the soldiers always come and haul the thief away to jail. My wandering eyes caught sight of teenaged Encarnación, who stood at a distance from the excited crowd, his head bowed sulkily.

I'm pretty sure he is our thief; he's so embarrassed he hasn't come by our house in days. A naturally curious, outward-thinking boy, I see him hanging in the balance between growing up to be lively, social, and spiritual like P.J., or a drunken small-time pilferer like many of the river Pumé. Amazingly, theft is a shameful aberration to the savanna Pumé, happening very rarely. I hope growing up in a traditional village like Doro Aná will help keep Encarnación honest.

8/3/92   The news from the village of Yagurí is that Pancho and Juana Trina's sick baby has recovered! Whether it was our medicine, the curing ceremony, or both doesn't matter; I feel more cheerful than I have in days.

This afternoon Rusty got back from a hunting trip with a fat tegu lizard. These lizards, called *ipurimechá* in Pumé, are about two to three feet long and very muscular. They have sleek bodies covered in shiny checkered black skin and powerful heads with ferocious jaws. We butchered ours and popped it into the pot, a clawed forefoot sticking rakishly out from the rim. The tail is my favorite part, the sweet white muscles parting from the vertebrae with just enough reluctance.

8/8/92   Yesterday Trino, who has moved with his family to a small temporary village to the south, shot the first deer of the season, a big buck. He sent boys with hunks of venison to share to our camp, and we lost no time in stewing it up. I had a cold and was lying in the mosquito net, so Rusty did the cooking. The meat was delicious, so fatty and tender it fell off the bone. As we licked our fingers, we noticed purple-black storm clouds boiling up out of the east. Rusty, who didn't feel like walking in the rain out to the trash pile, threw the deer bones into our dying fire just as P.J. strolled into the house to visit.

His big smile vanished and his eyes popped out of his head as he saw me munching and Rusty stirring the bones into the coals. "Hey, bury those coals!" he yelled, gesturing. "Put a cloth over the pot!" Bewildered, we stared up at him.

Just as the words left his mouth a lightning bolt struck the edge of camp a few feet from our house. The ground shook and the

itchy smell of ozone filled our nostrils. The Pumé went wild! Women whooped, children shrieked, men shouted, and P.J. ran out into the storm, frantically singing, blowing blood, and whistling to chase the clouds away. María Florenzia and her three little girls, who live next door, came scurrying over like frightened quail and huddled on our floor next to me, shivering.

After the storm had passed, P.J. sat at our hearth surrounded by excited Pumé. He explained that lightning is a living being, very hungry. It especially loves the blood and bones of deer, lizard, anteater, and armadillo, and if you put those bones on the fire the lightning will smell the smoke and strike your house. If you want to chase lightning away, P.J. advised, burn the bones of fish, crocodile, or electric eel.

Neither Rusty nor I can believe this actually happened. First, we've never had deer here; second, we never throw bones in the fire; third, lightning has one chance in a million of striking right at the edge of camp! What a meeting of coincidences . . . I guess we've just helped fuel the Pumé belief in lightning magic for the next hundred years. I might believe in it now myself.

8/9/92   Yesterday Francisco killed a cayman, a small South American member of the crocodile family. The *arí*, as it's called in Pumé, was about five feet long; her dainty snout with its protruding teeth and her golden eyes, half-closed in death, were primordial-looking. Her body armor of scutes was covered with gray-green skin splotched with glossy black stripes and spots. The meat is snow-white, sweet and slightly rubbery with subcutaneous fat that releases itself nicely into broth. Cayman eggs are covered with a soft, leathery shell, and after boiling the yolks are dense and granular, the whites never hardening but staying lacy and semi-transparent. Scrumptious.

8/11/92   Francisco, the young capitán of Doro Aná, is very dark with cheekbones so wide that his face is diamond-shaped. He has a habit of standing outside in the early morning scoping out the weather, his hii over his shoulders and hands clasped regally behind his back. He is everything I admire in a person with authority: kind, honest, adamant in defense of his people's interests, slightly aloof with adults but playful with children. He is the best hunter in camp and very generous, as I mentioned earlier; his girls are always sharing out food from his wife's hearth.

I've seen Francisco in furious confrontation with ranchers over an alleged cattle theft. I've seen him happy and tired after a long hunt, or a day in the garden with his wife harvesting bai. I've seen him toss his dignity aside, shouting and playing tikirí with the young boys and tickling babies. He often comes over to visit, sitting with his daughters climbing all over him and chatting with me in a friendly but decorous manner, as befits our relationship as in-laws.

His wife María Florenzia is light-skinned and slender with a long face and prominent teeth, like her mother Lucrecia. She is "little sister" or *anyikuí* to me, but stays fairly aloof. If she's not cooking, she's sewing, weaving, or doing endless piles of laundry. But while she's not as social as some of the other women, she can't hide her curiosity about us, and seldom loses the chance to peek at whatever I'm doing. Often at the end of the day, when we're both hot and tired, she looks over, girlishly blows a strand of hair out of her eyes and surprises me with a luminous smile.

Her three girls, Ramona, Olga, and Manisanta, are strong, healthy, beautiful, and high-tempered as well as popular. The happy result of María F.'s expert motherly care and tireless work, they can often be seen running and yelling through camp; they are Pumé kids at their best. And from the way María F.'s belly is pushing out her dress, I'm guessing she's pregnant again.

8/13/92   By listening to the women I've just figured out the se-cret of their nicknames. Nicknames can be very useful here. If a woman wants to call out to someone who stands in the relationship of big sister to her, she can just yell, Hey, Amí! But that way three women, all "big sister" to her, might answer. The Pumé prefer not to use their Spanish names (which they view as solely for foreigner use), so they solve the problem by calling each other by a modified form of their children's names. Chita's mother, then, is Chitaranyí, Docha's mother is Docharanyí, and so on. I think the *-aranyi* part might mean "the bearer of." I'm pleased to have solved this puzzle, and I often use these nicknames in my notes.

The other day María Diachi and her husband Victor were on their way out of camp to go gathering when I saw them both bound off the trail as though they'd stepped on a snake. They shouted in high voices and everyone came running. Just outside of camp was a large, bathtub-shaped patch of burnt earth, surrounded by dead, yellowed grass—the spot the lightning had struck a few days before. Everyone circled around, keeping well away, as though expecting lightning to shoot out of the ground. Since then, two groups of visiting Pumé have been shown the spot and told about our epic blunder with the deer bones. The Doro Aná people will dine out on this damned story for years.

8/19/92 In the quiet moments before I fall asleep, or when I'm by myself during the day, I find myself thinking of home. When I'm in a good mood these memories taste sweet, and I chew them contentedly like cud. But sometimes the memories taste like bile, like heartburn, good things turned bitter in my belly and rushing upward to make me feel lost and helpless here. Today, luckily, I'm in a bovine mood.

The water is receding slightly; hiking no longer requires struggling through thigh-deep water, but the savanna is now mostly ankle-deep, thick black mud, like good brownie batter. The grasses, tender jade green in June and deep reginal emerald in July, are growing tawny. The layers of the horizon as seen from our house go from dun sand to bright green weeds, golden grasses, heavy dark green treeline, and finally the sky.

Today the sky is blue-gray enamel from approaching storm-clouds to the north. The colorful layers of scenery are sometimes punctuated by startlingly white egrets, a foolhardy deer, or Pumé coming and going with baskets, shovels, or bows and arrows. As I watch them, the breadth of the llanos envelops and mutes the colors of their clothing, and the main color I see in their tiny distant figures is the glowing orange brown of their skin.

8/23/92 This late in the wet season we're not eating much, just as in the transition period between dry and wet seasons. Game is very scarce, and we're surviving almost wholly on what the women bring in or process, mainly wild roots and tambái cakes. I've lost a fair bit of weight this wet season, and as I lie in the burí I can see all the new cords, knobs, and twisted cylinders of my legs surfacing as the fat recedes.

8/27/92   A few mornings ago Eulogio, carrying a bow and arrow, walked up to one of the little chickens he's been raising so carefully. While it pecked obliviously at the ground, he aimed straight down and shot it point-blank with an arrow. After an astonished *Bawk!!* the chicken was picked up and whirled around to break its neck, then quickly plucked, butchered, boiled, distributed, and eaten in the space of a few minutes. Rusty and I couldn't help bursting into laughter at the sight of a common chicken being taken by surprise by a Pumé bow and arrow.

This morning Eulogio walked to the well with a bucket for water because his wife Docharanyí is weak from a bad cold. On his way out, he dumped some of the old water onto little Chita, who was sitting peacefully in the plaza. She gave an aggrieved yell, and when I laughed Eulogio caught my eye and laughed with me. He has a cannonball-shaped head, perfectly round with very slanted eyes, a narrow-bridged hawklike nose, and thin curved lips. He is short and very dark-skinned with the powerful muscles of a Pumé man in his prime, about 40 years of age. He is a good hunter and fisherman, and a busy gardener.

At his age Eulogio is old enough to be his little girls' grandfather; I like to watch the family at tohé, when this powerful older man with so much unconscious dignity in his bearing sits regally in his chair. He is constantly bedeviled by his two daughters, who climb all over him like kittens on a Newfoundland retriever.

The girls Docha María (since the Pumé can't pronounce r's and s's, her real name would be Rosa María) and Domana (Romana), are about four and three years old, respectively. They are the naughtiest kids in camp, and have the bad habit of peeing right in the middle of the plaza, to the disapproving yells of the adults. Their mother Docharanyí's face is triangular, pretty but worn, with permanent wrinkles between her eyebrows. This is probably because she frowns at her girls often, and is the only adult I've ever seen slap her children (if they were mine, I'd tie a rock to each one and chuck 'em into the creek).

Usually, though, Docharanyí is very tolerant. I've watched her do her laundry or make tambái with infinite patience in the face of the most horrendous kid tantrums and misdeeds. Sometimes she will just pick up an angry daughter and tickle her, or chase her around waving a stick until both of them are screaming with laughter.

8/28/92　Docharanyí's big sister Amelia has always fascinated me. The elder of P.J.'s two wives, she has the habit of standing at the edge of camp on firmly planted feet, gazing off into the distance with her head held high on the perfectly straight column of her back. She is always the first to spot interesting things in the distance, and when her eyes aren't animated by annoyance, curiosity, or laughter, there's always that far-seeing, sailor's look in them.

Besides having her mother María Diachi's firmness and purpose of movement, Amelia is an able, hardworking gatherer and weaver and is undisputed queen of P.J.'s household. Her co-wife and little sister María Luisa serves as a handmaiden and constant companion to P.J., attending to the lesser chores of the house and garden work while maintaining her hair and clothing as fussily spotless as is possible in a Pumé camp.

Still, Amelia is a lonely queen. She had a baby boy, Batida, about a year ago and P.J. doesn't sleep with her anymore. Sometimes Amelia will fake falling sick just to have her husband pay a little attention to her.

Batida is the prettiest baby in camp. His skin and scalp are firm, and satiny the way a baby's should be, with no sores or infections. His hair is thick, black, and glossy, and his huge almond-shaped eyes are brilliant black and lively, absorbing everything quickly. He cries very expressively, and I can always tell his mood, whether he's hungry, or being teased by his big sister Marina, or feeling sick, or just being fussy and wanting to annoy his mother. Amelia is tireless in her efforts to cadge a little extra soap for him, or a little extra medicine. His father P.J., the main healer in camp, hovers over him and sings healing songs to him even when he isn't sick. He is a gorgeous baby and his parents are taking no chances with him.

8/29/92   My first day free of a month-long cold and the weather is helping me celebrate with dazzling sunshine that picks out the silver in the roof thatch and makes it shine like shaggy sheets of mica. Each green leaf in the garden throws up its silver reflection to the eye, and after a brief rain everything dances and sparkles in the fresh wind. The black clouds receding on the horizon highlight the landscape by setting it off against their curdled darkness.

Juana Trina has come to visit with her baby girl, the one who was so sick last month. I was stunned to see, instead of a little brown spider, a healthy, alert infant clinging strongly to her mother's hip with chubby legs, looking around her. I couldn't help choking up; it was like watching someone return from the dead.

So, of course, now it's Batida's turn to fall sick, and we're treating him for the symptoms of a cold and that familiar villain, diarrhea. The beautiful infant of last month is weak and crotchety, dropping weight and losing his abundant hair, which worries me. Just think—every adult Pumé has to weather this kind of illness every year of their lives, and most of them have lost sisters, brothers, parents, children, and mates on this rough road they're born to walk. Every Pumé person I see is a miracle of toughness and survival, however pathetically they may exaggerate their illnesses in order to bum a few more aspirins.

9/1/92   Everyone has lost so much weight from when I arrived in April. The firm, rounded brown arms of the women are thin now, the sagging skin covered with insect bites and sores. Everyone's face is hollowing out, eyes retreating into sockets, cheekbones jutting out, jawbones standing out from the neck. Even the teenaged

girls, who during the dry season are actually a little pudgy, are now thin and lethargic, and older people like Victor and María Diachi and nursing mothers like Chitaranyí are so thin they look like completely different people.

9/2/92   With the turning of the season a few new plant foods are turning up; José just trotted in with a couple of pieces of boiled squash from the garden for us. The squash, called *edé*, is beautifully speckled, striped green and gold like living marble on the outside and a glowing orange on the inside. The flesh is nutty, rich, and sweet, and you can drink the broth after boiling it.

The Pumé are now harvesting some hard corn, with kernels like little white teeth, grown in tiny patches in the gardens. If you roast it, the corn becomes golden underneath with an opalescent sheen that rapidly turns a pearly black and explodes, *POP!*, if you look away for too long. It is sweet and very chewy. Sadly, the poor soil makes corn difficult to grow, and the deer and rabbits eat most of what does grow before the ears are ready to harvest.

Chokuí roots are wild, but are encouraged to grow in the gardens. They are shaped like teardrops or fat little fish, and are covered with a delicate fibrous peel. The white flesh is firm and crunches like a water chestnut when eaten raw. Boiled chokuí look exactly like little onions, slightly pearly and translucent, but in taste they are everything you like in new potatoes compressed into a single delicious bite.

As days flow by I scribble away in this journal, feeling a devouring anxiety to describe everything that happens out here, not to let anything slip past. In the long, dark nights that yawn before me I lie sleepless, whispering to myself long passages to write down in the morning. How can I put the words down so that this world will come back to me when I read about it at home? It seems like I could fill dozens of pages with the thoughts that fly through my head each night, but like passenger pigeons they darken my mind's horizon only to go extinct in the dawn.

The Pumé huddle in their houses waiting for an evening storm, which paces and growls off to the east. P.J. is whistling and talking to it. The children run and play in the darkening plaza, their high voices hanging in the still, thunder-oppressed air. Rusty sits in his chair combing lice out of his hair; the cold silvery light on the side of his bearded face could be from a New England window.

Travels and Travails
in the Late Wet Season

SEPTEMBER–OCTOBER 1992

In which we travel down the Meta river; Doña Petra;

baby capybaras; a squalid frontier town; San Fernando

again; blessed food and phone calls; my first river

dolphins; Pumé Christmas; horrible tiny fish stew;

a gruesome infection; roasted mouse; Gusha;

chúchu's; chokuí in transition; a harrowing birth;

an early death; our new daughter

9/3/92   The other day I was settling down to grate bai for tambái cakes when young Ronald from Don Armando's ranch shouted at us from across the creek. We sloshed over and found out that the ranchers were making their monthly trip into town for supplies, traveling up the Meta River by motorboat. We'd been waiting for weeks for an opportunity to go to town, and happily accepted the ranchers' offer of a boatride.

After a long hike to the ranch, we loaded up on beers and a delicious criollo supper of peppered fish hash, rice, noodles, and cheese. Moraima, the young woman married to Don Armando's son Chi-chi, did all the cooking. She watched us with a Mona Lisa smile as we ravenously scooped huge piles of food into our mouths. Afterward we waddled, belching, to our room and fell into the hammock.

We left in a long launch with an outboard motor before dawn, sliding out onto the big river under a blaze of stars. Don Pedro, a Pumé riverboat pilot, started up the motor and we headed down-river with old Don Armando sitting regally in a porch chair amidships, his thick glasses speckled with spray. We noted with satisfaction that he was wearing a brilliant yellow rainslicker, one of the gifts we'd brought for this generous ranching family.

In front of us the salmon-colored dawn hurled itself out of the water to hang glowing on the horizon. The trees, festooned with vines and creepers, crowded the banks like an audience. Little green parrots flew over us fanning the air with busy pats of their wings, and the occasional snowy egret or blue heron floated half-seen and silent through the trees. Crowds of slovenly, tousled-looking green and red parrots lounged in the overhanging branches.

After picking up three more passengers and traveling all afternoon, we stopped at the ranch of Don Armando's friend, Doña Petra. She is middle-aged, short and stocky with frizzy hair (hinting at Caribbean ancestry) and tiny black cheerful eyes. Every time I glanced at her, I caught her staring at me with healthy curiosity. She kindly slipped me a delicious, soft molasses cookie ("They're called *catalinas*," she whispered) and a piece of sweet bread, or *pan dulce*, tactful comments on my skinny appearance.

Under the tree in her yard were tethered two baby capybaras. The adults are the largest rodents on earth, weighing over one hundred pounds and swimming South American rivers and swamps in search of water weeds. These babies were about the size of rabbits and looked like coarse-furred, long-legged guinea pigs. Their heads are big for their bodies, with worried little eyes and crisply wrinkled ears set near the top of the head, so that they can hear and see while nearly submerged in the water. Their little toes are webbed for better swimming. The babies were shy at first but liked me to rub the bridges of their noses, and made deep stuttering purring noises.

The criollos tell us that in the sixteenth century the Pope declared that capybaras are fish, and are therefore permitted to be eaten during Lent by South American Catholics. Rich, pungent capybara meat is very popular, and during Lent they are rounded up and slaughtered in the wild by the thousands, since efforts to domesticate them have failed. I was sorry to think that these appealing babies were being raised to be items on the Lenten menu.

The next day we took the boat to the first town this far up the Meta River, called La Lechuga. It's a depressing little frontier town full of poor criollos crowded together with Pumé and Guahibo Indians. The Indians are better clothed and fed than we've seen so far, but they are stoney-faced and grim when they're not falling down drunk.

It was deeply disorienting to see a paved road, telephone wires, billboards, cars, and trucks. We got on the bus to San Fernando and I caught sight of my face in the rearview mirror. It looked thin and foreign to me.

Our first time in town in six months: the heat rising from the pavement, the traffic, the noise, the greasy smells, the high heels and pantyhose. Grubby and exhausted, we wander dazedly through the streets carrying our packs. Passersby stare and smile. We check into a little hotel, drag ourselves up the stairs, and take cold refreshing showers. Still in a state of shock, we wander to the bakery and walk out with all the chocolatey, coconut creamy, covered-with-sprinkles pastries we can hold. Back in the darkening room we sit naked on the little bed and gorge on the pastries one after another, laughing at each other as we spill crumbs on the sheets.

9/6/92   The days in town have passed quickly in a blur of governmental offices, little stores where we buy supplies, and, gloriously, *restaurants*. Each evening we devour huge meals of criollo food that leave us gasping for breath and reeling through the hot, dark streets clutching our throbbing bellies in deepest distress. I look like a spider with my skinny limbs and bulging stomach.

We've managed to call our families on the primitive Venezuelan phone system. It was so good to hear their voices, even blurred and distorted by crackles and whistles. Just talking to my mother and father makes me feel strong again, as though an empty spot somewhere inside me has been satisfied. I feel rejuvenated, and although I'm having a good time in town, I'll be glad to get back to Doro Aná and see how our gang are doing.

9/11/92   After a few extra days in town we left on the boat again, weathering a huge storm huddled in our raincoats and holding our faces downward so we could breathe. In the calm afterward the river boiled with fish, and excited birds including giant kingfishers, egrets, herons, and cormorants dove into the water all around us. Above the pandemonium sailed curious parrots. The giant red macaws, as long as a person from head to tail, looked like mythical dragons with their flamelike tails streaming proudly behind them in the blue air. Their chattering voices and fiery colors faded into the trees as they left the river's edge.

I spotted a few caymans and a capybara sliding off the banks into the water, and began to get sleepy. As my eyes stared blankly at the sun-glazed river, I saw something gray and gleaming slice through the water and heard a gentle sigh. Before I could blurt out, "A dolphin!" another one surfaced and dove. Suddenly all around the boat dolphins swam, blew, and sported, throwing their sparkling bodies out of the water in joyful play.

Freshwater river dolphins only live in three parts of the world: India, China, and South America. They are large, about nine feet long, with broad winglike flippers and strange faces with slender, beaky noses, sharp teeth, and tiny eyes that have almost lost their sight due to the muddiness of the waters where they swim. The ranchers traveling with us couldn't understand why I was so excited, but smiled tolerantly as they told us the creatures' Spanish name, *tonina*.

9/16/92   The Pumé met us at the ranch to help us carry our supplies. They looked so thin and dark next to the criollos! We marched into Doro Aná and opened up the bags, with everyone crowded around talking. We gave out tools, pots, clothing, and food. It was a Pumé Christmas.

After everyone had cooked, shared, eaten, and packed all their new goods away, people relaxed in their hammocks or groomed each other. Docharanyí and Eulogio sprawled gracefully like lions in the slanting evening sunshine while their daughters climbed, played, and fought on their recumbent bodies. Some of the women came over to our house, and María Diachi sat next to me on the ground, going over my head with the little wooden grooming tool, the *topaté*. Unlike Rusty, who is gentle, old María pops nits with sharp jabs to the scalp that make me wince.

9/18/92   As the fish, who spawned in May, grow bigger, the Pumé are going after them enthusiastically. The water level is dropping as the wet season ends, and tiny isolated pools are filled with fish the size of large minnows. A fish poisoning plant called *bi* is grown in the gardens, and the Pumé remove the leaves and sun-dry the stems and roots. When someone spots a pool with fish in it, people grab their machetes, baskets, and bunches of bi, and run out to swish the bunches around in the water. They then thwack the dying fish with machetes and scoop them into their baskets.

Rusty and I are stunned to see the Pumé taking fish that weigh about as much as a handful of paper clips. Nowhere in the literature of anthropology are people recorded as bothering with such small game. Since these tiny fish are impossible to gut and their bones are small, you have to eat them whole. The Pumé munch down these bitter, prickly morsels with every sign of deep enjoyment. However, Rusty and I have finally found a Pumé food we just *can't stand*. When a smiling Pumé comes over with a bowlful of tiny fish, Rusty's face is a study in forced politeness. He smiles stiffly, accepts the fish, and we gag them down, sneaking whatever we can't finish out to the grass for the waiting dogs.

One of the blisters on my foot has become infected. Infections out here are a very serious matter; simple things like bugbites, blisters, or small cuts can swell, turn red, ulcerate, and burrow down to the bone. At times the Pumé, especially the children, get sores that cover their arms, legs, and heads, expanding and deepening mercilessly as their victims scratch miserably at the itchy edges. But the Pumé immune system is very strong, and with a little help from our antibiotics the sores haven't been too gruesome this wet season. On the other hand, Rusty still has deep, dark scars from infections he contracted during his 1990 reconnaissance.

My blister had gotten so bad that yesterday it covered most of my heel and made walking impossible. Then my whole leg became involved, aching all the way up to the crotch, which really made me nervous. I finally realized the antibiotics weren't going to do the job, and I bit the bullet and slit the ping-pong-ball-size blister with my pocket knife. Struggling not to vomit, I drained the pus, which took over five minutes. But I can hobble a little bit today.

9/19/92   Cats wouldn't do too well out here in Pumé country—all the mice in camp are eaten by hungry Pumé kids. This morning María Florenzia's little girls spotted a tiny mouse with sandy golden fur, beady black eyes (and very bad luck) in their house. Manisanta chased it into our house and I chased it back out. Then the girls chased it back in and I caught it under a cupped hand. I handed it by the tail to Manisanta, but she was so surprised that it was still alive and wiggling that she dropped it and the chase started all over again. To the sounds of excited shrieks and breathless laughter I caught it again and stunned it carefully, and the girls ran away to kill and roast the tiny creature, which can't weigh more than an ounce, in the coals of their mother's fire.

9/25/92   I am struggling to learn how to weave, but so far all I've managed to do is squint at the mats and play with a bit of rag I've cut into strips. The old women are no help, laughing at my clumsy attempts with the rag strips. There is apparently no particular way to learn a skill out here. "Just do it! Just learn!" the women insist.

A late wet season bath: I walk across the savanna with the sun sparkling and trees dancing in the late afternoon wind. I carry soap, a towel, fresh socks. Flocks of parrots fly overhead chattering noisily, black against the sky, jade green against the trees. The doró writhes in its bed like a snake of cool glass; I lie in the current and stare at the pale green feathery fronds and the brilliant rust-red leaves of waterweeds as they wave sinuously under water. They brush my body with its skin palest silvery green, and the young fishes nibble at me, who will in turn soon be nibbling at them.

Yesterday I sketched Gusha weaving a hammock. It's frustrating to draw out here; the bugs bite your hands and the Pumé are never still for more than a few minutes at a time. This time I managed pretty well and was rewarded with Gusha's husband's praise: "That is good, really good."

Gusha is about twenty, her face smooth and oval with pouting lips and a straight nose. Her eyes are very dark, with fine eyebrows in an inverted V above each one. Her skin in the dry season is flawless, but her smooth plump brown arms are currently a bumpy landscape of gnat bites. Her hair is black and luxuriant—the thickest in camp. She keeps it in a shiny fat braid but at dance she often lets it cascade loose. She is the best weaver in camp; her mats and baskets are exquisite and tightly woven. Her house is as clean as a Pumé house can be, despite the constant presence of her infant stepdaughter. She herself has no children, and I think she's using a contraceptive plant I've heard mentioned.

The little girls keep pestering me to see my breasts, or *chúchus.* Every few days I unbutton my shirt and they whisper, "How white they are! They are so little!" Then they put their little hands on me to make sure that my chúchus feel the same as their mothers'.

10/2/92   I went gathering chokuí today with Docharanyí. We harvested in the dappled shade along the edge of her garden, and I was astonished to watch her stack the stems while she dug the roots. When she exhausted a patch, she carefully replanted the stems, patting the loose earth with her hands. Looking around, I could see she'd done this with several patches, and they all were growing vigorously.

I watched her with a sense of awe, seeing through the mists of time an ancestress similarly crouched over a wild root patch with her digging stick, thinking to herself, "If I replant these stems, they might spread and I'll have a bigger patch next year . . ."

It's very cool and rainy, and the wind is blowing. Creamy gray clouds encircle us on every horizon, promising storms with softly pulsating thunder, and the women huddle, wrapped in their cloth *hiis* for warmth while they groom each other. I wonder idly what the Pumé would think of snow.

10/5/92   Yesterday morning I returned from another chokuí gathering trip and found our house torn to pieces, the medical kit looking like a bomb had hit it. I looked nervously around for Rusty, remembering that María Florenzia, hugely pregnant, had gone into labor the night before in a temporary camp about a mile to the south.

Rusty was nowhere in sight—no note, nothing. Camp was deserted except for the family of María Llovina, who'd been gathering with me, and I didn't understand a word they told me. In a panic I set out for the other camp, which I'd never visited. Of course I took the wrong trail and realized a mile later I was headed too far west. Fighting back tears of fear and frustration, I struggled through waist-deep water toward a tiny cluster of huts perched on the crest of a sand dune.

When I arrived I could see a small group of thatched houses on the crest of the dune, and a tiny brush shelter standing at some distance from them. A crowd of Pumé were standing around the shelter, Rusty among them. María Florenzia was inside, squatting on her heels like a statue, holding a tiny red baby, wrapped in cloth, in her lap. She'd been squatting that way for about ten hours, since the labor had begun.

The baby's umbilical cord stretched back into María Florenzia; no one was willing to cut it yet. The old women were wailing softly, wiping tears away with the backs of their hands. My heart froze; I've never seen the Pumé cry except when people are dead or dying. Rusty dragged me aside. "It's twins," he whispered. "Something's gone wrong!" We bent over our little medical book and looked up twin births: "Get the mother to a hospital IMMEDIATELY," it advised helpfully.

We decided I should try to feel what was happening inside, and I squatted next to María Florenzia in the tiny birth shelter, lifted her dress, and felt her huge belly. Rusty had not been allowed to examine her, as the Pumé do not feel it is proper for a strange man to touch a woman. I don't know what he ultimately would have done if I hadn't been nearby.

I felt a large bulge, probably the head of the baby, positioned under her right breast. The baby was wedged diagonally, probably shifted by the labor contractions from the first birth. We decided I should massage the baby into a normal breech, or feet-down position, which isn't as good as head-down but seemed to be our only chance.

Rusty left to wait with the men, and most of the other women drifted away. María Florenzia's husband Francisco was in the traditional seclusion of husbands whose wives are giving birth, sitting alone in one of the houses and saying nothing to anyone. María's brother Pedro Julio sat at a small fire a few hundred yards off singing softly, probably a healing or birthing chant.

I've never had any medical training. I tried not to think about that, nor of María Florenzia's probable fate, a horrible lingering death, as I began to massage her belly. Her mother Lucrecia and mother-in-law Rufina looked on, wiping their noses.

I'll be able to feel María's dry, warm taut belly under my aching hands for the rest of my life. There was blood all over her, pooling in the sand below her; the rich rusty smell of blood filled my nose along with the musk of her sweat. After grunting and straining over her for an hour (during which she was bravely silent except for a moan or two), I let her lie down and take painkillers with plenty of water. While I watched her rest, I was aware that my shoulders throbbed and my hands felt like claws. It seemed we'd made a little progress; the baby almost seemed vertical now. But when I scrubbed my hands and carefully probed María Florenzia's vagina, I couldn't feel a thing.

María Luisa, little Manewi, Lucrecia, and Rufina stood or squatted patiently while I took the opportunity to examine the first baby. She was tiny and plum-red but perfectly formed, with the square jaw of her father and grandmother. She was beautiful and tough; she'd been lying for hours unable to nurse because her umbilical cord wouldn't stretch far enough and the Pumé were unwilling (for reasons of their own) to cut it.

Rufina prodded me. "Do that some more," she said, miming my massaging. "Yes, yes, get on with it!" Lucrecia insisted. The old women had guessed what I was trying to do. "Get up, little sister," I said gently to María Florenzia, who clutched her first baby as they lay together in the bloody sand. "I'm not ready, too tired," she complained in a whisper. Her face looked like a skull—her cheekbones stood out like little shelves and her eyes had retreated far into their sockets. But under the merciless pressure of the old women she struggled back into the squatting position and I took the baby, cradling her in one arm. Lucrecia, who had collected *toh pundéh* (the leaves used to dye women's loincloths and as a cure for female complaints) crushed and mixed them with water, smearing them on her daughter's belly. Then the old women helped María Florenzia balance, one holding her up under each armpit.

Suddenly I saw a purple, glistening mass covered with veins bulge out of her—the baby's feet still encased in the placenta. I looked around wildly for a place to set the first baby in order to free my left hand. I turned to María Luisa, who stood by watching. "Take her! Take her!" I shoved the baby at the young woman, who backed away, smiling uncertainly. I started yelling in a high-pitched voice at her, and the old women, in spite of themselves, giggled. In desperation, I propped the first baby on my left thigh, crooking my left elbow around her so she wouldn't slip off. The waters broke, there was blood and mucus everywhere. I reached in, gently tucked the coming baby's arms into her chest, and she slid out into the daylight.

A tiny, powder-blue baby lay in my hands. María Florenzia sighed and the two grandmothers said, "*Hamboá, hamboá.*" Dead. I put my lips to her little mouth and tried to resuscitate her, but she had probably been dead for hours. The women sent Newe for something to cut the twins' umbilical cords with and she returned with a piece of jagged rusty metal from the trash heap. Horrified, I hurled it into the bushes and used my clean pocketknife to sever the cords. The first baby was finally free, and while María Florenzia held her close, the rest of us sat back on our heels and cried.

The bloody afterbirth and placenta lay together in the sand next to the dead baby, whose little square-jawed face was asleep and blue, her arms and legs spread to the gently waving branches of the shelter and the blue sky overhead. A *paintó* fan lay nearby and the thought that she would never learn to weave one tore my heart out.

Young María Luisa, who had been so useless a few minutes before, scolded me into walking down to the bathing pool to wash myself. I was bloody up to the elbows and had blood and mucus all over my face. After I'd walked down and washed myself, I saw Rusty and Francisco approaching. They squatted quietly nearby while old Rufina, still wailing, told one of the girls to get a cloth from the house. I was told to put the dead baby onto a small rag, which I did while Rufina helped me tie it up.

Ramona came back with a bigger piece of cloth. Fittingly, it was a towel Rusty had given to the family as a present two years before. The grandmothers directed me to lift the little body into the larger cloth and tie it into a bundle. María Luisa began to dig a deep, square hole nearby, and I put the little bundle in it as the old women told me, with the baby's head facing west. Rufina talked softly to the dead child while I worked, but I couldn't hear her words. She then helped me fill the tiny grave with soft, sweet-smelling sand and we punched it down with our fists. Several of the girls had fetched heavy branches, and we placed them over the mound to keep off scavenging animals.

The old women told me to dig another hole for the placenta, afterbirth and bloodstained earth, which I buried carefully. I gently told María Florenzia to move aside and she did, never looking up from her lap. Lucrecia picked up a stick and shook it in the air over her living granddaughter, who was lying quietly in a cloth on the ground. She spoke softly to the baby, then held her left arm out palm upward and stroked the air above the arm with the stick, still talking. Her daughter María Florenzia finally allowed herself a moment of terror, pain, and exhaustion and slowly crumpled to the ground, huddling there with her face hidden in her hand.

We took the birth shelter down around her and rebuilt it a few feet away on clean sand. To my astonishment, María actually picked up the baby, stood shakily, and walked without help to the new shelter. I gave her painkillers and an antibiotic, told her I was leaving, and that I would be back soon. Then Rusty and I walked up the hill to give extra medicines to Francisco, who sat tired and grim in his hammock. Rufina, ever the practical grandma, gave me a load of bai roots to carry home. The familiar weight of them on my head was very comforting as we started hiking home through the flooded grasses.

On the trail I was exhausted. I couldn't stop shaking and kept tripping over my own feet. When we were out of sight of the houses, Rusty turned around suddenly and crushed me to him, his shoulders shaking with sobs. "You saved María's life," he whispered. I set down my load of roots and we held each other for a while, standing knee-deep in the water, not speaking.

As we walked into camp, everyone stared. María Diachi, normally so critical, came into our house and beamed at me. P.J., who had run home with the news ahead of us, also came in with a big group of people and described events for the boys and other men, who hadn't been there. He spoke loudly and pointed at us with pride, his eyes sparkling with the excitement of the story. When people left the house, I stumbled down to the little bath hole and washed off the last of the blood in the setting sun.

10/06/92   I've been adding to the October 4 journal entry as bits and pieces come back to me. We visited María's family yesterday and were treated to the sight of Francisco's broad smile; everyone was doing well. María Florenzia quickly handed me the tiny baby girl, already wearing a little dress sewn by her mother. The baby is unbelievably small, about four pounds. The stump of her umbilical cord has dried up and been snipped off, and she looks to be healing well. Her mother says she is sucking well and her little mouth opens and closes easily, showing no signs of tetanus or meningitis.

Her eyes aren't open yet, but she has abundant silky black hair on her head with wisps of down on her arms, legs, and cheeks. Her skin has lightened from purplish red to rose-petal pink, soon to darken to the coffee brown of her sisters. She slept soundly while I looked at her. Already I feel especially close to her. In the Pumé family structure this child, the daughter of a woman I call little sister, is my daughter, too. I told her in Pumé that she needs to grow up so she can go out gathering pará, chokuí, and yipái with her grandmother. Everyone chuckled and the sun sparkled on the grass blades as they danced in the wind.

As I write, I am still in shock over this. I'll never be sure if María could have made it without my help. All I know is everyone had given up and was mourning her for dead when I arrived. I did my very best; I did what anyone else would have done. With a dead baby stuck inside her, María Florenzia would have died horribly, she'd be dead this morning. She helped me by being patient, trusting, and strong as an ox. And now we both have a new daughter.

GRASSLANDS TO BIG CITY,
WET SEASON TO DRY SEASON

10/08/92   After another visit to the south camp to check on the new baby and her mother, we were invited to Trino's house nearby. His whole family had moved over to this short-term village to help Francisco and María Florenzia's family to care for the new baby and harvest bai from the southern gardens. I can't get over how mobile these people are; they seem to move house every few weeks for a visit, or fishing, or gardening.

I liked sitting down with a big gang of women to help them process bai. It was nice to sit there, sifting flour amid a crowd of busy, chatting, yelling, laughing, baby-tending Pumé women. I felt more like family than I ever have before. Afterward we hiked back home through a new crop of brilliant magenta flowers, nodding like clown's faces in the waving grass. A storm reared and pawed away to the west as we struggled through the mud like ants in melted chocolate.

10/11/92   Francisco and María Florenzia have just moved back here, and camp is lively with young Olga carrying her brand-new little sister around from house to house. Most of the people here are getting their first look at Doro Aná's newest member. As Olga makes the rounds followed by admiring little girls, I can see the bright pink soles of the baby's feet bouncing where they stick out of the swaddling cloth.

Her mother's belly is still sore and she is very gaunt, but her skin looks healthier and her eyes are brighter and more alert. She looks light and cheerful after the long, hard pregnancy. And one week after nearly losing her life in childbirth she had walked over a mile in the tropical sun across the flooded savanna, loaded down with her baby and a heavy taiyó full of her household belongings. María Florenzia, I take off my hat to you.

10/13/92   Today a ferocious storm blew up suddenly out of the northeast and practically blew kids and dogs off their feet. Francisco walked quickly to Eulogio's house, where Eulogio helped him pierce his tongue all the way through with a sting ray spine. Francisco flinched about as much as I do eating a hot chili. He then stood in the middle of the plaza surrounded by whirling darkness and spatters of rain, and spat blood at the storm, shouting at it to go away.

He spotted a little dog, Cheteníra, crossing the plaza and called her over. Frightened, she belly-crawled over to him, but to everyone's surprise he pulled her standing by her front feet and blew blood right in her face. After he let her go she tore around the plaza, growling to herself in an ecstasy of joy. And as we watched, a ragged blue hole opened in the savage clouds above camp, which stayed miraculously bone-dry while the storm raged all around us.

10/15/92   The new baby's eyes have opened. The silver bloom is gone from the irises and she can apparently track my finger as I wave it in front of her face. As I held her and talked to her she stared at me with vague alarm out of those huge brown eyes, the biggest I've ever seen on a baby. Then she made a few squeaky comments, kicked, and peed a tiny puddle on me.

10/19/92   The day before yesterday I went on my first hunting trip with Eulogio, his wife Docharanyí, and her big sister Amelia. We set off very early and headed west, straight into the savanna with the grasses waving in the vast morning distances stretching before us. When Amelia nearly stepped on a poisonous pit viper she bounded off the trail like a deer and Eulogio cautiously shot it with an arrow from about six feet away. He held up the dead snake on the point of the arrow to show me, and we both made "blecch" faces, our eyes squinting, tongues sticking out. Then he chopped the snake into little pieces with his machete, blew on the corpse and spoke to it, and set fire to it.

We continued west, Amelia gathering a few roots and Docharanyí encouraging her old shepherd dog, Oncha, to look for rabbits. Keying her voice to a high pitch, she would urge, "*Hu! Hu!*", Pumé for, "Sic 'em!" Oncha, good dog that she is, flushed a fat female rabbit that Eulogio killed with his first shot. He nailed the rabbit while it was running about ten yards away, right through the eye.

We turned northeast and fanned out in a big line, the two women searching for yipái roots and Eulogio for game tracks. He caught a male armadillo, and the women dug yipái steadily. It began to get very hot in the blazing, brassy sun, and I glanced at Docharanyí. She is seven months pregnant and the long trip had begun to tell on her; her face looked thin under its shining veneer of sweat, her bedraggled hair in her eyes. She noticed me looking at her and smiled wearily, probably guessing at my concern for her.

Amelia was about fifty feet to the west of us when she noticed a big tegu lizard, or *ipurimechá*, sunning itself on a termite mound. Quickly Amelia pointed it out to her dog, an inexperienced pup much younger than Oncha. The pup merely ran around in confused circles with her nose to the ground, and Amelia dropped her basket and bounded off after the lizard through the hummocky grasses, her heavy square-bladed shovel held at shoulder height. The glossy, two-foot-long black ipurimechá vanished into its burrow and Amelia began digging, quickly reaching the water line and shoveling up dark gray mud.

We could see the lizard's muscular body in its beautiful checkered black-and-gray skin, writhing powerfully as it tried to evade the sharp blade of the shovel. Amelia expertly killed it with three blows to the head and hauled it out carefully by the tail to whack it once more on the neck; ipurimechá have big jaws and sharp teeth and can inflict a bad bite. Then the two of us marched back to Docharanyí, who had watched the whole thing from a distance. I was exhilarated to watch a woman hunt, making successful use of her digging tool to excavate for and kill prey.

We harvested yipái for the next few hours and caught up with Eulogio, whose catch now included another ipurimechá, a baby tortoise, and a tiny lizard called *chirurí*. He'd made frequent stops to light fires, which help clean up the dead, tangled grasses left over from the wet season, now nearly over. We divided up the game, with Docharanyí getting the rabbit and the armadillo, and Amelia getting everything else.

As we trudged home through the fierce heat, Eulogio joked with me, saying, "I'll bet you're pretty footsore (*hurutú*) by now!" "Just a little bit," I joked back as I limped along behind him. We had walked about ten miles through mud, sand, and water without a bite to eat that day.

10/20/92   In our sixth month here, even the dogs accept us as family; their daily friendliness cheers me up and reminds me of my two dogs at home. A few days ago Francisco and María Florenzia's clownish, spotted Chibúka came out to meet us while we were visiting. Instead of barking as she does with Pumé visitors she doesn't recognize, she laid her ears back, wagged and smiled as she escorted us to the doorway.

And yesterday while I bathed in the little bath-hole, the pup Cheteníra wandered down to lie in the grass and keep me company. When I clicked my tongue at her to come back with me, she was so pleased that she growled and play-bit my ankles all the way up the trail.

Gonzalo just got back from a long hunting trip with several ipurimechá, and he generously gave us one to cook for ourselves. After I'd boiled it in lightly salted water the meat was more sweet, tender, and fragrant than anything I might spend a fortune on in a gourmet restaurant. And even better, it was free, it was alive only an hour ago, and it was eaten outside in the clean air and golden late afternoon sunshine.

How can I ever go home to a city again? I feel that living out here has dilated my eyes and I can see so much more now through my new pupils—new joys and new terrors, beside which all the old extremes fade away. I can't remember how good Chinese food tastes, but then I can't remember what it feels like to fear rape, or murder.

10/22/92   Yesterday I went on a long root gathering trip with Lucrecia, Diacricia, and Rufina. At the end of the day, we hiked home through the flooded grasses bordering the doró, the old women loaded down with sixty or more pounds of roots in their open baskets. Diacricia caught her foot in a snag and sprawled headlong into a puddle, but miraculously kept her brimming baskets balanced on her head so perfectly during her fall that only four little roots fell off the top. Awe-stricken, I helped her get up and gently placed the spilled roots back in her basket.

10/23/92   We are due to travel back to Caracas, the capital, in a few days, and I told Rusty I'd like a little break at the ranch for a couple of days before we headed to town. He helped me pack and I set out this morning, my first solo trip to the ranch. On my way out, Dori came running after me, calling, "Amí! Amí!" When I told her why and for how long I was going, she made the crying gesture with her hands wiping at her eyes. "We'll cry without you here," she said. Touched, I promised her again I'd be back soon.

I was hailed by a few more Pumé on my way, and had to tell my story a few more times. But soon I was on my own in the vastness of the yellow-green *chirí*, or savanna. Worried about being able to find the right trail, I turned my mind off and my feet found the way. Baby fish flew along the flooded trails in front of my boots, and caracara birds, their white crests ruffled by the hot wind, glared at me with crazy yellow eyes rimmed with red.

When I trudged into the ranch's front yard, the men were digging out a coconut tree stump. They seemed amazed that I'd come over by myself. Don Armando, in particular, was full of smiles, shouting "*Mujer! Mujer! Adelante!*" ("Woman! Welcome!") and pumping my hand. Later, Moraima asked me shyly, "Weren't you afraid, walking all that way by yourself?" "A little," I told her truthfully.

Silmari, the daughter of one of the women helping Moraima with the housework, is about eight years old and has abundant, curly brown hair, a pointed chin, and big, sparkling brown eyes. She is lanky, charming, devouringly curious, and delightfully straightforward. After a brief courtship she has become my bosom buddy, and I help her with her alphabet as we sit at the table on the porch. Sometimes she comes into my room when I'm reading and climbs into the hammock with me, bringing her doll. She is patient with my clumsy Spanish, and, childlike, unafraid to correct me when I use the wrong word.

10/24/92   As I sit here watching the men drive the horses out this morning, I think about how much I've changed since coming here. Becoming used to so many strange things has been like going through childhood again. Only the longer I'm here, the stranger things seem, and the more there is to explore. Is that why some old people are so easy about the world? Learning not only to accept one's ignorance, but to embrace it?

My ignorance here blossoms forth in richer, more brilliant colors and flavors, goes deeper, wider, higher. It explodes slowly like a supernova over the months and years, while I nibble away at its expanding edge, tottering with uncertain steps toward the ever-receding center of understanding. Accumulating facts merely ornament the growing circumference of this big ignorance of mine.

Sunrise is very pink today, a pure pink like sugar or alcohol, and the last ghost of a morning fog coats the grass and encircles the trunks of moss-covered trees. The deep roaring of the howler monkeys down by the river is muffled. A flock of egrets, tinged rose, flies over the freshly whitewashed house.

A hummingbird is busily making its morning rounds in the enormous mimosa tree's tiny, flame-orange blossoms. This tree, probably older than the ranch, is one of my favorites, its shade always cool, breezy, and hospitable to the hot, footsore traveler. A huge ceramic cistern of red clay with a bulging belly and coated with lichen, made by the river Pumé, sits on an old wooden platform under the tree. Two cups on nails invite you to drink the cool water inside. Strange purple and white orchids grow just above in the crotches of the tree, which is home not only to hummingbirds but lizards, bats, parrots, huge mantises, and butterflies. The long brown pods of this tree contain hard seeds and a sticky sweet syrup, a favorite snack of visiting children. No wonder Pumé mythology has a life-giving, food-giving tree at its core.

10/25/92   A fellow anthropology student from Spain, named Gemma Orobitg, came visiting to the ranch this morning. She has been living with and studying a group of Pumé in Chenchenita, a community of about one hundred Pumé settled permanently on the Meta River. The government supplies them with a school and a little medicine, and surrounding ranchers often hire Pumé workers for their fields.

According to Gemma, life with the river Pumé is completely different from our situation with savanna Pumé. Like the savanna Pumé, the river Pumé once were mobile hunter-gatherers. Due to their proximity to the river and incoming Venezuelan ranchers, the river Pumé have become more and more acculturated to the European way of life, and are familiar with permanent settled lifestyles, agriculture, domesticated animals, trade goods, and cash currency.

The river Pumé have access to clothes, a little medicine, and much more food than the savanna Pumé. However, they suffer much more from various diseases related to their settled, overcrowded living conditions. Worst of all, the constant availability of alcohol has created high levels of drunkenness and its handmaidens: violent assault, child neglect and abuse, and chronic illness. I can't imagine how different it must be to work there.

Gemma, about 27, is willowy and elegant, her brown hair always tied back, pretty earrings in her ears, her clothes always spotless. Next to her I feel acutely conscious of my patched, stained clothing and big boots. I have forgotten most of the Spanish I learned earlier this year, as the Doro Aná Pumé don't speak it, and while I can communicate roughly with the ranchers about food, laundry, and other small concerns, it is a whole new ball game to talk shop with a fellow anthropology student. Luckily Gemma, who wouldn't be out here unless she had a lot of guts, is very sympathetic and apparently happy to meet another woman student. We talked all morning on the sunny porch, with young Silmari peeking curiously at us from around the doorway.

Rusty arrived with our going-to-town baggage, and Gemma offered us a ride to La Lechuga in her motorboat. So we'll be leaving a little earlier than we'd anticipated, but it's nice not to impose on the ranchers again. It is cloyingly hot today, and the gurgling roar of the howler monkeys down by the river seems to be the heavy voice of the humid heat itself.

10/27/92   We left the ranch at dawn two days ago, with a full crew of Pumé and a few of the ranchers too, including Chi-chi, his wife Moraima (all dolled up and cheerful for town), and their baby girl Amanda. Riding with us were a young Pumé mother and her two-year-old girl, who is riddled with tuberculosis. Gemma, noticing the child's steady decline, had radioed in to the Indian Affairs Office asking for transport to the capital and treatment for the little girl. She was told, "Sorry, we don't have the money." So Gemma is bringing the mother and child into town herself and will be paying for everything out of her own pocket. She told me, "I'm tired of watching children die!"

The little girl has lost most of her hair, can't walk, has ulcerated skin and a huge tumor on her chest. The contrast with the glowingly healthy Amanda is incredible. Still, the sick girl was curious and alert, and grabbed at me, smiling just like any Pumé child. I am rooting for her.

When we arrived at La Lechuga, wilted from the long, hot ride, we were surprised to meet a boiling crowd of people, all waving sticks and bows and arrows. We were ordered to land on the south side of the river by their spokesman, and we obeyed, cowed and confused.

The protest, which meant a boycott on all travel north, was against a proposed national park, which will encompass a huge section of the Meta River area. The Park Service appeared to have forgotten to solicit the opinions of the criollos and indigenous peoples who had been living inside the proposed park boundaries for decades, or perhaps thousands of years.

Amid an angry crowd of people of all colors and sizes Gemma argued that they couldn't detain us, we had a very sick child with us who needed help right away. There was a shouted conference and the child, along with Gemma, her mother, and an older Pumé man scheduled for a hernia operation were finally allowed to cross the river to the road north. The rest of us were told to get away from the boat, as we wouldn't be allowed to cross until the government revoked the park decree.

We milled around in the crowd, which seemed to be composed of excited, self-important protesters, frustrated travelers, and the usual fringe of drunks who will wave a stick and yell whenever an opportunity presents itself. Almost immediately we were pounced upon by a group who asked us if we were National Park employees. We told them we were not, silently praying they wouldn't go through our permits, which indeed includes one from the park service. After we repeated ourselves several times, the men seemed appeased, but seemed to think we looked so much like scientists (i.e., the enemy) that they asked us to pose in a newspaper photo. We agreed uneasily.

Suddenly we were enclosed in a circle of small, fierce-looking men, mostly local Guahibo Indians, who took aim at us with their bows and arrows. With the characteristic criollo mixture of ferocity and antique courtesy, the protesters assured us nothing would happen to us, everything was perfectly safe, it was just for the newspapers. The journalists, smiling brightly, snapped our photos and the crowd dissipated. I surreptitiously checked myself to make sure I hadn't wet my pants.

A comic interlude ensued when we bumped into three German tourists, likewise stranded by the strike. The three women were dressed in goofy Euro-trash outfits consisting of tight, brightly colored leggings, arty T-shirts, Birkenstock sandals, cat's-eye sunglasses, orange hair, and shocking red lipstick. Oh, and of course, big cameras.

The poor things, with the arrogance characteristic of German tourists everywhere, had ventured into the deepest, darkest wilds of rural Venezuela understanding no Spanish. They did speak a little English with us, though. "Zese Venezuelans, zey are so . . . *unfriendly*," they said, eyeing the seething crowd, which at this point had begun singing and marching around the plaza, waving their weapons excitedly.

Chi-chi and Moraima found us much later and arranged for us to stay with some friends. Already, food stores were running out due to the closing of the road, and we ate very lightly before hanging up our hammocks and philosophically trying to sleep in the sticky heat.

The next morning a group of women, including Moraima and me, attempted to cross the river in order to get at food and a proper kitchen to cook it in. Our men zipped us across the river and dropped us off amid the angry shouts of protesters on the other side, and we doggedly walked to a small shed and proceeded to cook a large meal. I tried to help as best I could and watched our menfolk gesticulating on the opposite bank as they tried to explain to the protesters. About a half hour later a boatload of protesters crossed over, landed near us, and boiled out of the boat.

Waving clubs, they shouted at us, asking us what we thought we were doing. The women put their hands on their hips and shouted back, We're trying to cook!, then stubbornly turned back to their pots. The defeated men, most of whom were drunk, rounded on me and yelled that I, at least, had to go back with them RIGHT NOW! So I shrugged at the women and walked back to the boat followed by the six men, all of them brandishing their sticks and scowling fiercely.

I had a packet of lemon cookies in my pocket and turned around, seeking to deflate the situation. "Have a cookie?" I asked politely. The hungry men stopped scowling. "Why . . . sure," said the fiercest one, in the yellow tank top. I solemnly handed out lemon cookies, and after many polite thank you's we climbed onto the boat and crossed, still munching.

After a long, boring afternoon we were aroused by the sound of a helicopter. It landed and disgorged the state governor himself, who blithely promised the townspeople he would quash the park. After riotous celebration during which Chi-chi grabbed his nearest neighbor and waltzed ponderously around with him, we climbed onto the truck and crossed the river on the ferry, free at last to head north.

10/31/92   In San Fernando we headed to the Park Service office to see what this proposed national park was all about. The skimpy, 39-page report simply proposed delineating a huge area of the river as park land in order to save endangered turtles and other species there. The multimillion dollar tourist industry would be welcome into the park, however, and special facilities would be built to accommodate visiting tourists.

The criollos would not be allowed to expand their ranches or farms in any way, and all buildings would have to conform to Park Service standards of rusticity to appeal to tourists. The indigenous people would only be allowed "traditional subsistence" (i.e., no modern technology would ever be allowed) within land allotments whose boundaries were not clear. Any park residents who disliked the rules would have two choices: leave voluntarily or be kicked out by the officials.

We were aghast at the extreme measures of the proposal. Nobody really knows whether they are necessary, or whether there *is* a possibility for a compromise between endangered animals and people who have lived in the area for generations. This park proposal beautifully illustrates the well-meaning but poorly informed approach of urban planners to rural issues, and for this reason it is bound to fail. For lack of a compromise, the fate of endangered animals still hangs in the balance.

11/6/92   Still shaking our heads, we boarded the bus for Caracas a few days later in order to renew our visas and permits, and buy supplies. After many hours on the stifling bus, we finally caught sight of the hulking skyscrapers of the capital marinating in smog. I gulped convulsively and looked over at Rusty, whose jaw muscles were clenched. Caracas.

In the chaos of the sweating crowds, booths, buses, and disco music that is the central bus station, I fought panic and watched the bags with an eagle eye while Rusty found us a taxi. I had forgotten how terrifying cities can be when you've been away from them for long enough.

The only hotel we could find that wasn't booked full was a snooty affair for tourists and fledgling diplomats, and the bellman looked us up and down and said, I am sorry, we have no vacancies. I explained to him that I'd called the day before to reserve a room and he made us wait outside while he checked at the desk. Finally, we were allowed to shoulder our bags and trudge, trailing the odor of sweat and dust, to the elevator.

11/7/92   We called Gemma, who has sufficient funds from her university to rent an apartment here, to check up on the little girl's progress. The child is in the hospital for treatment, and the Indian Affairs Office still refuses to pay or help in any way. A couple more Pumé have also come all the way to the capital, one a young teacher from Chenchenita and one an older man in need of a hernia operation. Gemma offered to let us stay with her and a roommate in her apartment and we gratefully accepted. We are down to our last couple hundred dollars, with nearly a year to go in Venezuela.

11/8/92   Pancho, the older Pumé man, is now out of the hospital and recuperating in Gemma's apartment, which has become a miniature boarding house and buzzes all day long with the sounds of Spanish, Catalan, French, English, and Pumé. Pancho, about 60, has grizzled hair and a humorous, intelligent face. He says he is related to most of the Doro Aná Pumé and we have fun gossiping with him.

Gemma took him to the zoo today and he was very excited to see familiar animals there. The jaguar, in particular, was the high point of the visit; Pancho said it was an uncle of his and that they had a long talk together while Gemma waited. What a strange scenario—a Pumé man and a jaguar trying to communicate through the bars of a cage, civilization wedged between the two of them.

11/14/92   Gemma says she has seen Pancho sitting up in bed, blowing on his own belly and chanting, trying to heal himself since there is no one else to do it for him. Although he possesses tremendous dignity and tolerance, he's clearly ill at ease in this huge city and chafing to get out. We understand perfectly.

11/25/92   After three frustrating weeks of traffic jams, expensive food, and uncooperative bureaucrats in the capital, we said goodbye to Gemma, who has been terrific. Since Pancho was unwilling to wait any more time in town, we agreed to "escort" him home to Sabanita, a small river community close to Chenchenita.

We took the bus to San Fernando and bought a few last supplies, treating Pancho to pastries and his own hotel room. He still hasn't learned how to walk in town, and instead of going side by side, he insists on tagging along single file. So we humor him, and I can glimpse the smiles of pedestrians as they watch us thread our way through the streets like ducklings, following an invisible trail six inches wide.

11/27/92   We have arrived at Los Algorrobos, a tiny ranching town west of Chenchenita, as the mayoress has offered us a free ride back to the Aguilar's ranch. I like this town; children play and shout in the sleepy streets, *joropo* music floats out of little adobe doorways, and cattle graze peacefully in the central plaza and in the mayor's yard. There's only one catch; we missed our ride and now have to wait for someone *else* to head out for Chenchenita.

12/3/92   Well, we hung around for two more days waiting for a schoolteacher from Chenchenita to sober up enough to get behind the wheel. Each dawn we'd be perched nervously on our bags, ready to go, and each noon he would stagger in, reeking of *aguardiente*, mumbling "*No es mi culpa, no es mi culpa . . .*" ("It's not my fault . . .").

So we whiled away the hours chatting, loitering, and avoiding Victor, a handsome young cowboy who apparently has a penchant for foreign women scientists. I discovered his feelings one night when, after a few beers, he trapped me against a wall dappled with moonlit shadows and declared his passion for me. I exasperatedly told him I was with Rusty, and besides I was way too old for someone his age. When he protested, I asked him, "How old *are* you, anyway?" "Eighteen," he replied with a heartrending sigh, his dark eyes regarding me meltingly through a romantic haze of beer fumes.

On the third morning we finally set out across the llanos in the back of Jesus Flores's old truck. Rusty, young Victor, a Pumé boy, and I perched high on a pile of baggage in the back, panting in the dry season sun, already hot at eight o'clock in the morning. For five hours we bounced, yawed, and baked along the horrendous pothole-pocked road. Victor kept trying to grab my hand or foot; sobering up hadn't dampened his passions any. I wonder if he does this all the time—it seems like a good way to get shot by a jealous husband.

The boat we'd arranged for from Chenchenita never showed up, but by great good luck Victor's brother cruised by in his fishing boat and agreed to take us as far as Sabanita, Pancho's home. We loaded ourselves and our bags and motored on into the antique gold sunlight of late afternoon, as it rapidly deepened into a nectarine twilight.

Trailing my hand in river water the temperature of milk, I noticed several small flocks of hoatzin birds in the darkening treetops to the north. These living fossils are the size of eagles, but are vegetarians. Their young actually have fingers on their wings like that feathered dinosaur, the archaeopteryx. Seen against the sunset their colors were amazingly rich and brilliant—I caught flashes of coppers, golds, greens, slate-blues, orange, and white. As we floated past them, they hopped awkwardly through the branches, erecting their crests with curiosity and alarm.

We got to Sabanita at dark and lugged our things up the steep bank to a cluster of tin-roofed Pumé houses. While the women and children giggled to hear Rusty and I talking in *Pumé máeh* (Pumé language), Pancho relaxed for the first time in weeks, enthroned in a leather chair.

The tin-roofed, permanent houses of the river Pumé are easier to construct and last longer, but we found them to be vastly inferior to the palm thatch houses of the savanna Pumé. For one thing, all sounds, from rainfall to whispered voices, are amplified, and the metal makes the houses hot at night. For another, the earth floor is pounded down so solid from long occupation that it's like cement; Rusty and I had to pound our mosquito net sticks in with our boots.

Yet the savanna Pumé are running out of palm trees in the limited area they are allowed by surrounding ranchers, and they too are beginning to use pieces of tin in their housebuilding. I was sad to think that someday the gentle hiss of rain on the palm thatch roofs, and their tawny silver beauty in the sun, might vanish forever from the llanos.

The next day was lost in a blur of getting ourselves and our bag-

gage to Hato San Jacinto, gulping down a meal, sleeping a few hours in the stifling heat, and hitching a ride in the truck as far as the doró. There we crossed, startling Corona, who was sitting quietly with bow and arrow in his branch shade, waiting for fish. In a minute more we were met by Victor, Luis María, and Luis Mende, who excitedly preceded us into camp. After the usual frenzy of the giveaway and a much-needed housecleaning, we crept into our hii and were dead asleep in five minutes.

The nights are becoming cool and breezy, and the mosquitoes and gnats are having a hard time fighting the incessant wind. I putter around our little house, do the laundry, straighten up my data notebooks, put the kitchen things in order. It's funny how I'm getting more and more used to this place.

The shock of transition from city to Pumé country is getting less noticeable, and it's really good to see the kids all growing, and Docharanyí's belly pushing out the front of her purple skirt. My little habí, or daughter, is flourishing; she has fat cheeks and a double chin, and her arms and legs are properly chubby as a baby's should be. Her family brought her over about four times yesterday and she grabbed my fingers, fussed, and peed on me as always.

Later, her grandmother Lucrecia came over and asked me if I'd trimmed my hair (yes) and whether I mightn't be pregnant yet (no). Then she took the baby and sat in a patch of sunlight with her. The old woman was so tiny and fragile herself that she looked like a child as she curled around the baby, rocking and crooning the Pumé lullaby, "Oooooooh riroh, riroh . . . "

12/4/92   The river is barely navigable by boat now, and our part of the doró is only thigh-deep. We can now bathe there, but it's hard to swim because the water is getting clogged with water-weeds. Also, the fish are getting bigger and less cute; a nip on the butt while you're bathing can send you yipping out of the water. Rusty has even more reason to worry! Although I'd expected the pirhanas swimming all around us to be the culprits, I was surprised to see that it's the *dapué*, a long-bodied predator, that are going after us. The little local pirhanas, called *apéi*, mainly nibble on the fins and scales of larger fishes.

The winds blow steadily all day long now, drying the laundry quickly, making dunes on our floor, getting dirt into the food, and spreading the fires lit by the Pumé and criollos alike to tidy up the dead grasses, which were waving breast-high when we left for the city. The brush has been burnt off around camp, and now short, thick jade-green tufts have sprung up that don't quite conceal you when you're crouching in the bathroom area a hundred feet out-side camp. Today a high, thin layer of clouds has muted the sun-light and brings a promise of rain. Together with the wind and short new grasses, the llanos feels as though someone has opened the windows and begun spring cleaning.

Many of the men are leaving on a big trip to Chenchenita, to participate in the vote for state government officials. Naturally, the Pumé have no idea why or for whom to vote, but in exchange for secondhand clothes or a small bag of rice they'll sign their "*x*" for any candidate. It makes my blood boil to think of those politicians cynically buying votes from the Indians, the poorest of Venezuela's citizens, whose welfare doesn't interest them in the slightest. But this practice is common, and is accepted by everyone as the status quo.

12/5/92   It is a windy translucent evening, softly gray and pink like the *hotokó* doves, who coo and throb to each other in the trees down by the creek. People are sleeping outside their houses now, although still in their mosquito nets, to enjoy the breeze. I spent the whole day making tambái and have stinging blisters on my hands, which have been softened by city life.

12/6/92   Holding the new baby, I realize that, for me, all the significance of birth, childhood, and death have coalesced in her tiny body. Despite her very real tendency to squawk and pee all over me, she keeps the mystery of her recent birth and brush with death clinging to her, pollenlike. I try not to think I won't be here to see her first steps, to hear her first words.

12/8/92   While Rusty and I were delivering a letter from Gemma to Don Armando at the ranch, we left some plant-collecting materials and all of Rusty's camera and mapmaking equipment we'd been using along the way in an old camp, where we thought it would be safe. As we hiked back from the ranch, our disbelieving eyes saw a thick column of smoke boiling up from behind the big hill in front of the old camp.

A Pumé must have been lighting the grass in the area, a prac-tice common now in the early dry season. Pressing ourselves to a jog, we arrived panting at the clearing, where we could see a smoking heap of glinting ashes where the plant press and the spe-cial case protecting the camera, binoculars, compass, and several rolls of film had been.

We are now totally at a loss as to how we are going to make maps and take high quality photos. Rusty is absolutely beside himself and I can say or do nothing to help. I can't believe the bad luck that has dogged this project—I feel like I'm trailing disas-ter behind me like a bad smell. I feel like running away. The Pumé sense our bewilderment and anger and are treading care-fully, only entering the house quickly to drop off food or get a little medicine.

I am mutely grateful for this consideration and try to thank them with smiles when poor Rusty can't find one. This afternoon he managed to play spiders with the little girls and I've never loved him more, when it took more courage to play with a couple of children in the face of his private disaster than to jump off a cliff.

12/9/92   My habí's name is Lucía Ana Josefina, or Ana for short. Her big sister Olga told me today when I was playing with them both. The other babies are all developing their personalities and relationships with us: José Raje will smile at me but becomes frightened if someone passes him to me; Dionisia María is as shy as her mother Miriam and never visits; Batida is cocky when his mother is around but otherwise very coy; and José Ahi is a little stranger living in the other camp, whom I barely recognize any-more. I hope little Ana continues to be comfortable with me as she gets bigger.

In my time off, I've been reading *Black Elk Speaks* by John G. Niehardt. Strangely, the Plains Indian way of life no longer seems

exotic or distant to me. It's only *another* way of life, existing inde-
pendently of time. I don't think my capacity for wonder has shrunk,
only that my ability to visualize other things has grown.

The introduction to this 1971 edition claims that the narrative
is "better than any LSD trip." It's a little poignant to think of all
those suburban-grown hippies, so young and bored, sucking the
book dry of its details like an orange. Trying to imagine a mean-
ingful life, a life lived in tune with nature and your fellow humans,
all that groovy stuff.

Those same earnest youngsters are now pursuing the Good Life
in any way they can; no longer having the time to grok on the Indians, they hold the good jobs in order to put their kids through
college and keep the house stocked with the latest appliances. It
would be too easy to scoff at them for their short attention spans.
Mine was short, too, until impulse and nearly blind chance landed
me here.

Francisco is taking nanú next door, getting ready for tohé tonight.
His hawking, sneezing, and retching make a nice counterpoint to
all this abstraction.

12/11/92   Two nights ago there was tohé, and I opted out while
Rusty went. Just after dark I was lying peacefully in my burí listening to the usual early tohé noises: children running, yelling,
laughing and crying; the big boys wrestling and yelling "*Ayah!*"
when pinned; women laughing, chatting, and shouting at the kids;
and men snorting nanú, sneezing, and gagging.

The singing had just begun when María Diachi's high, agitated
voice pierced the air. "Something's eating the moon!" she yelled
over and over. Everyone took up the shout, and fires were quickly
kindled. The men called out their storm shout, "*Ko ho!*" and pierced
each other's tongues in order to blow blood at the night sky.

Dori tiptoed into our house and whispered, "Big sister, the moon
is being eaten up! I'm scared!" She sat quietly down next to me

and was soon joined by Chitaranyí and her daughter Chita. I guessed it was a lunar eclipse, but I was reluctant to leave the house until I heard more. The fear was intense and contagious, and my palms began to sweat.

After a while, Rusty's silhouette appeared in the darkness. "It's an eclipse," he whispered. "Nothing to worry about." Then his voice broke. "I'm scared shitless!" He had been taking nanú with the men and was at the early, panicky stage of the drug when the eclipse began. I wormed my way out of the hii and walked out into a night of a million staring stars. The moon had been full, and completely eclipsed it was magnificent, a huge ball of gray velvet floating ominously in the northeast sky.

Some of the men were lying in their hammocks and shouting *"Bedawí!"* "Wake up!" to the dark moon. Other men and boys had run to a clearing just northeast of camp and were whooping and leaping, wildly waving flaming bunches of *hudí*, or thatch, at the darkened moon. Old Trino was out there with them, chanting a mile a minute and blowing blood. All we could see from the plaza were swooping, bobbing, or circling blobs of flame and the men's silhouettes, which looked like black demons cavorting in Inferno. Occasionally, a burning torch would be hurled up at the moon and fall back to the ground, setting small fires in the brush around camp.

Back in the plaza, a few of the women were singing along with Victor (who was giving tohé that night and not going to let a little eclipse interfere), or were sitting huddled in small groups, whispering and glancing nervously skyward. The moon stayed completely eclipsed for about an hour and was very slow to reemerge. I was surprised to feel real fear during the eclipse and relief at the moon's return, considering I hadn't taken any nanú and I know (on one level) what causes eclipses.

Today camp is quiet and sleepy with the dogs play-fighting, children singing, and the wind swooping through camp from the northeast, clouds of stinging sand in its wake. The sun shines fiercely down like a copper coin through a light veil of dust and smoke from distant fires. Spring in the llanos.

Sun, Birds, and Fish—
The Llanos in Spring

12/12/92   This afternoon I watch drowsily as María Florenzia prepares to bathe her baby daughter. Usually twice a day she will go outside the house in the sun with a little gourd bowl full of water, a cloth, and little Ana. María squats on the ground and scrubs the baby briskly using just her hand and the cold water. Ana squawks angrily and struggles, little shivers in her voice like a cold puppy's, but she is no match for her determined mother.

I can never listen to this ordeal without looking over, and the baby's helpless fury always makes me laugh. María is so used to hearing my stifled laughter next door that whenever she begins bathing her baby she pauses and glances over to make sure I'm enjoying the show. And when our eyes meet she always gives me her gentle, toothy smile.

12/13/92   I had a dream last night that I was again helping María Florenzia give birth to her twins. All the details were the same, only this time when the second baby slid into my hands she was pink. I wasn't expecting her to be alive and almost dropped her when she started to yell and struggle. Lucrecia and Rufina were laughing with joy, and I laughed too, to see that the family now had five daughters. I woke up smiling, only to remember the silent blue baby under the wind-shifted sands.

12/17/92   Nearly everyone has decided to disperse to small fishing camps nearer to the deep parts of the creek, in order to catch the fish concentrating there as the water level drops. Boys bring share-outs of big smoked dapué fish to us stay-at-homes, or hunks of smoked cayman, which is very tasty but has a texture like a spare tire.

The biggest babies, Dionisia María and Batida, are learning how to walk and stand. Their families plant sticks in the ground and stand the babies up next to them, showing their tiny, chubby hands how to grip. The babies respond enthusiastically, standing, walking carefully around the sticks, and sometimes falling down with a bump and looking around to see if anyone has noticed.

Pumé babies learn how to walk six to eight months earlier than babies in industrialized settings. The crawling stage is very short, about a month or two; Pumé babies are actively discouraged from crawling, and if they are caught will be helped to walk while holding an adult hand. My guess is that snakes, scorpions, and above all, dirt are rightly seen as dangers to babies and the Pumé want children up on their feet and off the ground as early as possible.

The first word the babies are being taught is *puá*, or bird. In the warm quiet evenings, over the children's laughter and the men's conversation, I can hear the women's coaxing voices floating across the plaza: "*Puá? Puá?*" and the babies' ". . . *puá*," more hesitant. Teenagers urge their baby brothers and sisters, "*Nyuwú!*" "Speak up!"

12/19/92   I had a pleasant focal session at Dori and Patricio's house this morning. After her husband left the house, Dori asked me if I had any babies at home. When I told her no, she asked, "Are you pregnant?" Nope. "Are you scared, then?" I said, "Yes, a little. I've had miscarriages." I asked her if she had any babies (there are no children in that house). She answered, yes, she'd had two, but both had died and now she was too scared of childbirth to try again. In Pumé, our conversation went like this:

> Dori: Bo gwaneh?
> Pei: Bo gwadeh.
>   D: Moéh? Moéhdeh?
>   P: Moéhdeh!
>   D: Uapámeh?
>   P: Buíchineh. Gwa kodí handí bo, hamboá akúru. Adóh menéh? Bo gwaneh?
>   D: Nyoní bo, hamboá, hamboá. Uapá kodí, bo eádeh!

It's an interesting challenge to write down Pumé, although it doesn't give any idea of the rhythm of the language, its stresses, the gestures and the eloquence of the eyes of the speaker. Dori is good for practicing my Pumé; she's a little shy, but we are closer than friends. Sisters.

12/20/92   Tiny ice particles hang high in the air above us, strangely undissipated by the blazing equatorial sun that beats down through the mists onto us. Rumors of Guardia Nacional soldiers being nearby scurry through camp, and everyone is tense with expectations of trouble.

Several families have returned from the small gardening camps to the south and the fishing camps to the east, and the little girls, reunited and reinforced, are being exceptionally rowdy. This afternoon a gang of them tore Eulogio's defenseless empty house to pieces, and Newe managed to pull down the kitchen shelf with all its stored household goods.

Teenage Encarnación, glowering, marched into the house and jury-rigged the shelf back to a wobbly stand. Now the girls are back inside swinging Manisanta in a burí, pushing her so hard that she's grazing the ceiling and the house is swaying to the sound of breathless, shrieking laughter. Maybe the roof will collapse on top of them.

12/22/92   Yesterday we hiked over to a neighboring criollo family's settlement to take photos of them with our last remaining camera. We were accompanied by a bunch of Pumé boys, all hoping for a little neighborly hospitality in the form of lunch. We stopped along the creek at one of the fish camps, where several families are still fishing, for some delicious fresh-smoked dapué.

The fishing camp consists of poles for hanging burís and a few brush shades where the women hang out during the hot, sunny days, tending babies and smoking fish that the men and boys bring in from the creek steadily all day long. The smoking racks, made of small poles tied together with vine, are only about two feet high. Underneath each rack is a fire of moist wood that will smoke a foot-long, fiercely grimacing dapué in about twenty minutes.

Fish can be eaten fresh off the rack, the delicious steamy flesh tasting of wood smoke, or they can be stored for a couple of days. I liked to see the Pumé so happy in their little camp on the wide savanna, in the wind, sparkling sun, and waving trees and grass. They looked so wild, free, and cheerful, the essence of mobile humanity.

Crossing the thickly overgrown doró, we came across Eulogio poised like a statue in a tree with bow and arrow, a few big fish already floating next to him by a dam he'd built. After greeting him we continued to the criollo Moleto's little adobe house, where we were treated to sweetened milk fresh out of the cow. The family scrambled to pretty themselves up while we waited; the kids ran to the pond to bathe and popped coyly into the house to change into their best clothes, while their big brothers changed shirts, combed their hair, donned huge sunglasses and *sombreros*, and saddled up the prettiest horses. A tiny burro was also caught and bridled.

All the boys posed on horseback, and their father Moleto also posed on horseback for a couple of shots with his 9-year-old daughter, beautiful and big-boned with lots of flyaway frizzy hair and the fierce eyes of a hawk. The whole family then posed behind the burro, the mother leaning her elbows on its furry back and pondering a dog-eared Bible, her eyes modestly lowered.

After the photo session we were all treated to a satisfyingly bulky lunch of rice, pasta, cornmeal arepas, and cheese. We then set off for home in a blazing hot afternoon, collecting a couple more smoked dapué on the way home. It never ceases to amaze me how two very different groups of people, the criollos and the Pumé, can live elbow-to-elbow like this. I really liked having a chance to see how the poorer criollos live; the Aguilars at the ranch, *patrons* to this and many other families, are unusually well-off.

Last night during tohé María Llovina brought her teenaged daughter Carmen Cartoria into my house along with María Florenzia's 10-year-old Ramona, and asked me if the girls could sleep with me. "All this talk of the soldiers nearby is scaring them," María explained. "Go ahead," I mumbled sleepily. After setting up burí and hii, the supposedly frightened girls whiled away the long hours of the night giggling, whispering, and calling various of their favorite boyfriends to come over and tell stories. Every half an hour they would wake me out of a deep sleep to whisper loudly, "Hey Auntie! Auntie? Are you awake? Aren't you scared of the Guardia? *Auntie!*"

This morning as I was groggily trying to collect household focal data, my mother Diacricia asked me if my chúchus held any milk. I patted my chest and joked, "Nope! I don't have any babies to nurse!" Diacricia smiled, then hauled her own wrinkled, brown breast out of her dress collar and squirted a stream of milk at me. I was flabbergasted, but then I've often seen old grandmas quieten babies by putting them to their own breasts. I had assumed it was just a dry pacifier, but it looks as if Pumé women can lactate well into old age and even nurse their own grandchildren!

Ana's gaining weight and her huge eyes are alert now, clear and a beautiful black like coffee. It's encouraging to watch her grow; she now looks like a miniature baby instead of an animated doll.

12/24/92   Last night we heard a spectacular domestic fight between Chitaranyí and Marcos Pala, the young couple who live next door with their two children. Chitaranyí accused her husband of sleeping around, raising her voice to a stage whisper punctuated with furious swats of the paintó fan against the wall of the hii. The whole camp hushed to listen, and Chitaranyí obliged us by pronouncing her words loudly and clearly.

Marcos Pala's weak defense was mumbled and inaudible. It apparently didn't make sense to his wife, either, because she threw him out of the house. He slunk over to grandmother Lucrecia's house to sleep, and is now staying in Rafael's little camp about a quarter-mile away.

Today Chitaranyí is walking purposefully around camp with her baby boy, well aware that people are watching her. Her determined tearlessness is an encouraging sign, because every time her wayward husband used to leave camp on his work jaunts for the ranchers she would weep wretchedly, aware that something was wrong. The men around camp have been joking about Marcos Pala being tossed out on his butt, and sympathy for him is at rock-bottom. I feel bad to see this little family, which had been struggling so hard, break up.

The girls are giving the daughter Chita a miserable time about it, and she's holding up bravely, glaring at them in their little whispering huddle and pretending she'd rather play by herself. My heart yearns toward the lonely little girl sitting proudly aloof with her crippled leg curled underneath her.

It is Christmas Eve in *Uí Aná Rupéh*, or across the Big Water. Rusty and I had a smoked dapué apiece tonight, and a few tambái cakes. I hope my blood family are eating well tonight. All the folks from the last fish camp have returned, and tonight's tohé promises to be noisy and exuberant.

12/25/92 Early this morning I wandered around bleary-eyed, putting together a fire, a pot of water, and a couple of precious teabags. As I built up the fire I noticed one of my gray heavy-duty hiking socks dangling from the section of the roof just above the hearth. Since I usually don't keep my socks there, I glanced curiously up at Rusty, who was brushing his teeth. "Hey, what's this sock doing in the roof?" I asked. Rusty, his mouth full of toothpaste, answered, "Why don't you take it down and find out?"

I pulled the sock down and inside it were a sun-dried piece of tambái and half of a smoked fish, its toothy mouth leering. Now thoroughly mystified, I asked, "So what is this *food* doing in my sock in the roof?" Rusty burst out laughing. "Don't you remember what day this is? Look, there's another sock up there. Take it down and see what's in it." I took down the other sock and shook out several pieces of charred wood. "That one's for me," he explained, putting on a long face, "because I've been bad and couldn't come up with a nicer Christmas present for you." But I made him share my Christmas breakfast with me anyway, and threw the charcoal back into the fire.

12/26/92   Lately, many of the young girls and women have adopted my ponytail hairstyle. It makes them look like Midwestern high-school students, but I think it's fetching. Also, it tickles me to set a trend in the Pumé fashion scene.

Chitaranyí has abandoned the little house she lived in with her family and has moved in with her grandmother Diacricia. Whenever Chitaranyí needs firewood, she strolls with elaborate casualness to her old house with a machete in her hand. I try to imagine her feelings as she strips the house that she built herself with Marcos Pala's help, and feeds the cookfires with it.

It's fascinating to me that, although two-wife marriages are not uncommon with the Pumé, *clandestine* affairs with another woman, without the consent of the first wife, are not tolerated. A second wife in the house has, if anything, a greater impact on the life of her co-wife than on her husband, and I suspect the reason co-wives are often sisters is partly because it works better when the two women have a previous bond between them.

12/28/92   The women have been complaining about the wet season camp wells, which are very low on water and stink of algae. Several families have moved about one-half mile north to a new

camp right near the creek. Eulogio and Docharanyí's family and Victor and María Diachi are now living in small branch shelters just west and across the creek from the first dry season camp we lived in last April. Now that the waters have receded, the creek banks are dry enough to clear and build on, and the rest of the Pumé families are sure to move soon.

I always like seeing Pumé on the move, their every belonging and usually a kid or two on their backs. The women, in particular, carry the heaviest burdens, and look like snails loaded down under baskets full of their household belongings. And so the seasonal heartbeat of the llanos pumps on: dry-wet, dry-wet, dry-wet . . .

It appears that the women, who are the main users of water and who do nearly all the well-digging and water-fetching, have the main say about when seasonal camp moves occur. The wells here have only a few inches of muddy water left in them, and woman-like, I too long to move to a place with clean, fresh water for our house.

12/29/92   Yesterday four letters arrived for me. I experience a sensation similar to hunger or lust whenever I see a new batch of these faded, water-stained, dog-eared envelopes with my name on them. My pupils dilate and my mouth waters.

Late last night Marcos Pala came running over from Rafael's camp with the warning that two strange men, possibly National Guard soldiers, were nearby. Camp surged to the occasion: while everyone packed their things, P.J. ran down and warned everyone near the creek, and they hurriedly packed their belongings in the feebly moonlit darkness and jogged back up here. Everyone sat or stood nervously in the plaza for a few minutes, counting heads and whispering. Nerves were jangled, and even the normally placid María Florenzia was spotting silhouettes of soldiers perched sinisterly in the shadowy foliage of her mango trees.

The men got their bows and large arrows and went out, fully armed, on a reconnaissance to the east. Rusty grabbed his flashlight and joined them. After about an hour of dry-mouthed whispering, we heard the men returning. Apparently, the two strangers on horseback had passed southeast of us earlier in the night. Rusty told me privately he thought they might be criollos out hunting deer.

But the Pumé, who have lived through several violent, sometimes deadly confrontations with these soldiers in this century, were ready to act in an emergency, the women and children fleeing across the savanna while their men covered the retreat with bows and arrows, their only weapons. It's not just history out here.

Such incidents are commonly brought on by ranchers complaining to the state government about cattle thefts. The Doro Aná Pumé fled to this location from just such an attack in the south some fifteen years ago. Amelia's first husband, Encarnación's father, was killed in one of these attacks, which remain unacknowledged by the Venezuelan government.

Today everything is quiet. Rusty and P.J. took axe, machete, and knives and are sweating their way through the construction of a big new branch shade for us down by the doró. We may move as soon as tomorrow.

12/30/92 And here we are! Early this morning we packed up and the Pumé men helped us carry our household belongings and equipment to our new branch shade, which consists of four sturdy poles planted in the ground and a latticework of leafy branches laid on top to form the roof. For the moment the *taréh*, or mosquitoes, are worse down here near the creek, but as the dry season progresses they'll gradually disappear. And the water here is lovely, cool and clear.

While we were busily packing our things this morning, an amused Rufina stood by to watch. Little Manewi was watching too, and tried to remind me I'd left something in the roof. She hasn't yet lost the unfortunate habit of calling me "*Niwéi nyí*," or female foreigner, even though she knows it's bad manners. But today I put my hands on my hips and answered her: "*Niwéi nyí deká!*" or, "No foreigners here!" Rufina laughed delightedly and added for me, "*Pumé kodí.*" I'm Pumé.

The birds are returning to our part of the llanos, flying south to escape the winter in the northern hemisphere, and this morning Eulogio bagged two great blue herons and three wood storks. While I sat in a pile of feathers writing about his butchering methods, he surprised me by handing me a small heron, its perfectly round yellow eyes startled and its beak agape.

"Um . . . I don't know how to cut these up," I said sheepishly. Chuckling, Eulogio took it from me and chopped it into stew-sized chunks in about ten seconds, and I scurried off with it to light the fire. Boiled up with a little salt the heron was fantastic;

I've never tasted such savory, tender bird, better than the best holiday turkey.

I can see the sky through the rustling leaves and branches that form the roof of our pretty new brush shade, and sunlight and moonlight dapple us when we're underneath. Because there is so much air and light moving through, the bugs can't light anywhere and don't haunt the shelter like they do our big wet season house. Although the hammock sags because the housepoles shift, and we can't figure out where to put all the dishes, I like it here.

The doró is lowering rapidly. The men have built a big dam of branches overlain with grass at the crossing near camp, which will trap fish as the waters continue to lower. We can now walk dry-footed across the creek along the top of the dam. We can also bathe in the creek five minutes away from our house, a real luxury compared to the thirty-minute excursions we were making from the wet season camp.

1/2/93   Today, for a change of scene, I followed a group of men out to *Ta Aná*, or the Big Lagoon, near Moleto's house, on a poison-fishing trip. Pedro Julio, Eulogio, Lui Mantini, Lui Mende, Juan Masano, and Rusty comprised the expedition, with me trotting along behind taking notes so that Rusty could fish. The morning was gorgeous, cool, sunny, and windy, like all our mornings now. We hiked past an encampment of Pumé working for Moleto, and past Moleto's house, pausing to say hello to him and his family. We then proceeded to the section of the lagoon where the road crosses. It is a narrow neck that is still under a few centimeters of water, but will be dry and passable by truck in a couple of weeks.

Trees and dense vegetation provide beautiful deep shade there, and the birds fluttered and called to each other above our heads as the men made impromptu dams to trap the fish. They then prepared the bi poison they'd harvested from their gardens in the

morning. First they pounded the tough white roots between logs, then stood in the water and swished and wrung the fibrous bunches over and over again. This poison, a variety of plant used widely across South America by indigenous groups and Spanish alike, works by blocking the air intake of the fish's gills similarly to the fish poison we saw used last April.

The cool, dark water yielded up gasping, glittering treasures of all sizes and shapes: silver disc-shaped pirhanas with bright scarlet fins and bulldog jaws; long, leaf-shaped silver and gold striped fish with pointed noses; gaudily striped and spotted black and white catfish with winglike pectoral spines; *pundichará* fish with rainbow and silver scales on their oval, flattened bodies shining like oil; dapué angry and gleaming green and pink, dorsal fins erect like the sails of warships, needlelike teeth bared; *yakará* gold-green with deep slate-blue vertical stripes, the peacock eye glaring from the tail and true eyes glowing brilliant crimson; and *cuiná*, or stingrays, their wings beef-broth colored with tiny black specks, furious eyes glaring, dangerous tails lashing and mouths working as they were dragged to the surface, yelling, "Gyuurk! Gyuurk!"

Eulogio, mindful of his hungry, enormously pregnant wife, kept on fishing after everyone else had quit, catching four more foot-long dapué. I was impressed at his skill in whacking them on the head with the back of a knife as they writhed and snapped, dangling on the hook; a fish that size can take off your fingertip.

Moleto invited us to lunch, and we talked with him while we munched. He said he thinks that the men on horseback that alarmed the Pumé a few nights ago probably are Marxist guerrillas from neighboring Colombia, who commonly make forays into Venezuela during the dry season.

These guerrillas are well known for kidnapping foreigners to extract huge ransoms from their families . . . oh well, there's nothing we can do. We'll just carry on and hope they pass us up as small game, which we are compared to the tourists, missionaries, and petroleum workers also present in this part of the country.

Later, P.J. and Eulogio assured us they'll drill any guerrillas that come near us. As always, P.J. was very expressive, mimicking an arrow shot through the heart, his hands miming the rhythmic gouts of blood and his eyes rolling, tongue lolling out sideways as his audience grinned appreciatively.

The Dry Season in Full Swing

JANUARY–FEBRUARY 1993

María Llovina; a guinea worm infestation;

naughtiness punished; weird fruit; struggling to weave;

our criolla neighbor Lu; Hollywood in the llanos;

jaguars on the move; a nanú overdose;

Marina gets a bum deal

1/16/93   Early this morning, while we were out of the house, María Llovina noticed our tabadá, or woven house mat, was about to blow away in the wind. She walked over and placed a hearth-stone on it, clean side down. Coming back, I noticed the stone, and as she smiled at me from her house I felt a wave of affection for her.

María Llovina is in her mid-40s and has a knowing face, al-ready seamed with wrinkles from smiling or squinting in strong sunlight. She is one of the only women in camp who always lets her hair fly free, and has the girlish habit of blowing it out of her face while she works. She is stocky in the torso and has very pow-erful arms, but her legs are like a teenager's, dark, slender, and smooth.

She has two daughters, one of whom (Carmen Cartoria) still lives with her. María has gone through many husbands; she likes young men, and since 1990 she has been married to two men half her age. Her latest, Juan Masano, is from the neighboring village of Yagurí. He is very tall, probably near six feet, with a strong back and dusky good looks.

When we first got here last April, María and Juan were in their honeymoon phase and more openly affectionate than most cou-ples; I liked to see them slapping and pinching each other, gig-gling like teenagers, or lying comfortably together in the burí during tohé dances. They've settled into domestic routine by now, but Juan still helps with household tasks like cooking and laundry, and accepts María's guidance in traditionally male jobs like gar-den clearing and housebuilding. Out of all the young men in Doro Aná, he is the only one with a garden, which was probably his wife's idea.

Both of them work really hard in their garden, and they are re-warded with a good harvest of bitter manioc, corn, and a little squash. María, like many other women, cultivates chokuí, the small potato-like wild root, in her garden. She instructs Juan to weed around the young shoots, and her chokuí returns are among the highest in camp.

María is always thinking up creative recipes, a favorite of hers (and ours) being squash chunks stewed in grated chokuí porridge. And when the food is done, María is the most generous sharer in camp. When I smell food cooking at her hearth, I know the smiling face of María or her young daughter will soon poke through the thatch of my house, accompanied by a warm plate in a brown hand.

María Llovina, more than anyone else in Doro Aná, understands us. "If I give a lot to these two," I can see her thinking, "they will remember it." She's right, of course. I'm always very generous in our trading and urge Rusty to be, too. María always offers good bargains and never forgets a debt.

She loves to smoke and gossip, is equally comfortable with men and women, and is respected by the former for her religious and political savvy and by the latter for her expertise in weaving, healing, and mothering children as well as her salty jokes. P.J. loves to stay up late chatting with María, calling out, "Hey, big sister!" across the dark house to start a long bull session.

1/18/93   A bunch of worried women came over to the house yesterday to tell us that Daí, the young wife of Lui Mantini, has "fly larvae" in her scalp, and that she is in pain. Mystified, Rusty went over to her house and found her suffering from three huge, swollen sores on her scalp. Each had a large white worm embedded inside, its hind feet serving as anchors and its head protruding slightly, blowing bubbles. Poor Daí's whole head was a reeking mass of encrusted pus, and my stomach turned as we examined her. The worms retract quickly when molested, which happens frequently as Daí's worried young husband relentlessly probes the sores with a stick despite our pleading with him to stop. His wife only winces and whimpers.

This morning Rusty smeared a mixture of tobacco extract and alcohol on the sores, along with an ointment that our neighbor Moleto says he uses on infected horses. This afternoon we can discern no movement at the mouths of the sores, and maybe the nightmarish things are dead. I've been eyeing Rusty's scalp and probing my own with my fingers; I don't know how you get infected but Rusty thinks it is larvae borne in the water, with which we daily wash our dishes, laundry, and our bodies . . .

Baby Ana is brought over to me now several times a day because her busy mother has only grandma Lucrecia as an alternate caretaker. This afternoon the baby girl slept peacefully on my stomach for a half hour as we swung lazily in the burí—it was nice to feel her tiny weight on me, in the wind and the shade of the waving branches.

Little Manisanta, Olga, and Docha María have just been pierced with the *cuiná buí*, or stingray spine, for exceptional naughtiness. The punishment, which consists of piercing a small fold of skin on the forearm, hardly takes a second but is accompanied by an impressive build-up: shrieks of terror, fury and humiliation, and frenzied struggles. All of camp watched and chuckled unsympathetically as each girl in turn was dragged over to P.J.'s house; he is the official piercer in this community.

Pumé kids are almost never disciplined; normally a growled reprimand will shame them into good behavior. But when all else fails, only a designated nonparental adult inflicts punishment, which probably hurts about as much as an ear-piercing. This morning while the little offenders destroyed the interior of a temporarily vacant house, they chose to ignore repeated warnings. Now they'll walk around sniffling and comparing the tiny wounds on their arms, and might refrain from truly horrendous behavior for maybe a day or two.

1/19/93   I went on a *ngoitóh* collecting trip today with Amelia and María Llovina and a few young girls. It was very pretty in the forest by Trino's garden, shady and overgrown and tough to walk through (for me, anyway). The women and girls dodged nimbly in and out of the brush collecting fallen ngoitóh pods like brown, pebbly oblong Easter eggs. On the way home we snacked on a few—you use a stick to smash the hard shell, and inside is bright green meat with the texture of a fibrous marshmallow. It is sweet and appley tasting, but one bite will suck all the spit out of your mouth.

Yesterday I collected four leaves of baby moriche palm and stripped the midribs off of some of them to make *bobuí*, the coarse weaving material for tabadá mats. The finer weaving stuff, called *go*, is the semi-transparent lower cuticle of the leaf. I hopelessly mangled several leaves trying to separate the go and pull it off.

Defeated, I wandered over to Lucrecia's house and shoved my last remaining leaf at her, explaining my problem. She gave me a big toothless grin, put down the tabadá she was weaving, and quickly stripped the little leaf I'd brought. Her hands moved so quickly they were a brown blur.

Holding up the soft, glistening fibers, she announced, "Handí gochí!" "This is how you strip go!" Then, with her typical generosity, she reached up and pulled down a bunch of her own go fibers from the roof, giving me a big bundle with which to practice my weaving, just as she would have with any earnest young Pumé girl.

1/21/93   Now that it is dry season we have criollo neighbors nearby that herd and milk Don Armando's cattle from the big ranch and make cheese all summer long. This cheese is the tangy, white, crumbly gold of the llanos, one of Venezuela's prized products. It is mostly produced by small families that migrate inland in the dry season with the cattle of their patron, then move back to the river's edge to work the fields in the wet season.

The mother of the nearest family, nicknamed Lu, is half-Pumé and has a longstanding relationship with the Doro Aná community. When she lives nearby in the dry season, she visits, trading and gossiping in pidgin Pumé, with our gang nearly every day. Lu is very stocky, with smooth creamy brown skin and beautiful high cheekbones she inherited from her father and has passed on to her children. Whenever she has extra milk, arepas, beans, or noodles, she drops by our house with a bright smile and a most welcome snack.

1/23/93   One of our friend Gemma's big projects when we last saw her in Caracas has come to fruition; she has managed to arrange for a French film crew to come to Chenchenita to film a Pumé tohé ceremony. The crew, who are very well funded, decided to take a flight over our village in their small airplane. As they buzzed camp, a spectacular fear epidemic exploded, with everyone running, shouting, and hiding.

Kondechará (fire chairs) is the Pumé word for any machine that people ride in, and flying ones usually mean the presence of the much-feared military. Amid the pandemonium, I glared up at the plane winking silver in the blue afternoon sky and thought that if those ritzy European filmmakers knew what kind of terror they cause with their little flights over picturesque Indian villages, maybe they'd think twice about doing this.

As I was writing the above words, the crew itself was bouncing over in a truck to say hello to us and to check out Doro Aná for filming possibilities. The Pumé, including even P.J., uncharacteristically stayed well away, whispering in a nervous clot on the other end of camp during the visit. As the light-skinned men and women in their latest safari fashions stared with ill-disguised apprehension at my manioc juice boiling on the fire, we chatted with them a little in English.

As always, talking to people makes them more likable, but I hope they decide against working here. They want to film tohé, but since they don't have night cameras they'd like to stage the dance during the day. To me, the very soul of tohé is personified by the beauty and secrecy of the night. Well, we can only wait and see. Whether they end up here or in Chenchenita, if these intrepid people have come all this way to film completely staged, artificial behavior, a daytime tohé will give it to them.

1/24/93 Two nights ago our criolla neighbor Lu and her kids came racing over in the dark, moonless midnight to whisper that a big animal was in the tree over their house. Lu said it was frightening not only the cattle, but the adult dogs as well. Lu's skinny husband Daniel was away getting drunk at the cockfights as usual.

P.J. and a couple of big boys armed themselves with bows and arrows, and using our flashlight they went over to look around. Finding nothing, they returned with Lu's mosquito nets and hammocks, and the family bedded down with the Pumé for the night.

Rusty and I think it may have been an adult jaguar on the prowl, as it's the only carnivore large enough to scare dogs away. Aside from the baby jaguar the Pumé surprised in a tree last wet season, we've heard nothing about the big cats except that, contrary to scholarly belief, they are a real danger to humans in our area. It would be exciting to see one from a distance, but a hungry adult prowling around camp is too much for me.

Baby Ana smiled at me three times yesterday while I was playing with her. It was shocking—she's really growing up fast. In another week or so, she'll be four months old. Little Batida and José Rahe are constantly in and out of the house, and 3-year-old Domana feels free to pester me as she would any Pumé adult. She'll swagger into the house with a devilish gleam in her eyes just I'm settling down to cook, write, draw, or sew, and her mother's yells in no way deter her efforts to climb all over me.

We saw our first scarlet ibis of spring yesterday, a single flaming note sung in the dark blue immensity of the morning sky. I wonder how good they taste.

1/25/93   Very late last night during tohé I was snatching a few winks of sleep in our house when little José walked in and asked me for water. "What for?" I asked sleepily. He answered, "Uncle is *niwí*!" By this I took him to mean that Rusty was in the elevated state (usually involving vomiting) brought on by the hallucinogenic snuff nanú. Since Rusty persists in taking nanú to be companionable with the men (against my advice), I chuckled and told José where the water was. When he returned with the empty gourd, he remarked, "Uncle sure is acting crazy . . ." "Yes, yes, now let me go back to sleep," I growled.

Ten minutes later Dori came in and said quietly, "Big sister, my brother-in-law is in great pain. You need to come out here." I flopped quickly out of the burí and hurried out to the feebly moon-lit plaza, where P.J. was singing melodiously. All the other men were gathered at the far end, holding Rusty upright. He was bone-rigid, with his arms outspread, his breath hissing through clenched teeth. He recognized me, told me he loved me, and then said goodbye with chilling finality.

Aghast, I ran to the house to get more water to splash on him, but when I returned he was completely flipped out, howling and screaming in English. Rafael and Corona, both mature men who have seen a thousand such bad nanú trips, supported Rusty on both sides as he slumped in the dirt, sometimes rubbing it in his hair or his face. Only the men and the old women dared come near. Lucrecia and María Diachi took me in hand. "Get in there and tell him, 'I'm here!'" they ordered. I held his hand, gray with dirt, and said loudly, "*Piyí kodí*!" Rusty's uncomprehending blue eyes continued to glare at some vision behind my right shoulder.

Trino crouched and blew blood from his pierced tongue onto Rusty's belly, which the older men had bared. It only seemed to agitate him further. He continued to yell and whisper, talking alternately to his dead father and the Pumé ancestors or the Old Ones (*Ote Tí*). He grabbed the men around him to emphasize points, and the Pumé put up with it good-naturedly, although he was speaking in English and they couldn't understand a word.

After an hour he calmed a little, and we walked him over to his burí, where he sat awhile, tired and confused but still talkative. The men stayed near for a while, and when they saw he really was coming out of his trance they filtered off to dance and sing. A few of them returned periodically to talk to him and hand him cigars to puff.

María Diachi and Lucrecia told me the nanú was a weird batch, and several other men had had a rough time that night. Rufina kindly brought over a bowl of fermented manioc punch for Rusty to drink, and it seemed to revive him a little. Dori and Amelia, two of the braver young women, came over and sat near me as if to comfort me with their silent presence. Meanwhile, P.J.'s beautiful singing continued in the fading night, the women in the chorus replying piercingly. Kids approached cautiously to see if their uncle was okay yet. I stayed near for another hour, then left him to calm down with the Pumé for the rest of the night.

In the dim, cloudy dawn I rejoined him in the burí outside and P.J. came over and sat down on a stump next to us. He made sure that poor Rusty, by now completely exhausted, had plenty more *bai eró,* or fermented punch, to drink. Trino and a few of the older men assured Rusty that they'd been sick as dogs, too. Before everyone wandered off to a well-deserved sleep P.J. turned to us, his tired face lit up by a mischievous grin. "You know, that was the *really good* stuff!" he chuckled.

We spent the rest of the day quietly, bathing, washing clothes, and lying in the burí. It was windy and cool with sprinkles, a lovely pearlescent day. I told Rusty flatly that I'll leave if he does nanú anymore. I just can't go through that again; the drug is rumored to kill people by stopping their hearts. Rusty agreed to swear off for the rest of our stay. It's common for Pumé men to abstain for up to a year after a scary trip, so they'll definitely understand. I feel somewhat reassured, and tonight we'll both sleep like the dead.

1/27/93   It's been three days since the film peoples' visit and they show no signs of returning. Although nobody's said anything, I think the Doro Aná Pumé share our relief. The river Pumé are accustomed to constant interaction with ranchers, traders, and government officials, but out this far on the llanos the Pumé are much shyer.

Yesterday our criolla neighbor Lu came over with her teenaged daughter Marina and two of her younger boys. The family was out of food, and Daniel, who was supposed to have gone to the ranch to get groceries, was nowhere in sight. I gave Lu a stack of tambái cakes I'd just taken off the fire, and the children immediately began munching on them, thanking me with their eyes. It was nice to help them out for a change . . .

As always, when visitors are in our house the little Pumé girls come over and stare defiantly at them. Newe, in particular, is very possessive, hanging all over me and playing with my hair. Lu noticed her and remarked, smiling, "*Te quiere mucho*," or, "She really likes you." I was pleased that she noticed.

My weaving practice has caused a lot of amusement in camp lately. A couple days ago a gaggle of women were sitting in my house, and María Diachi said to me, "Hey, take out your weaving!" I pulled it out of the roof and handed it around. Amid the soft chuckles I heard one woman say, "*Pumépa*." She's doing it the Pumé way, she's becoming Pumé.

As I sit writing I can see pregnant Docharanyí sitting peacefully in the sunshine outside her house. She is wearing a purple dress and looks like an eggplant. I wish I could know when the baby will come.

1/28/93   With the coming of little squalls of rain everyone is building miniature wet season houses with thatched roofs. The airy branch shelters are still used on sunny days. Rusty, P.J., and Francisco built us a small house too, and it's nice to be able to hang our things in the roof again instead of on flimsy branches. It's the only way to keep things safe from marauding dogs, chickens, bugs, and kids. After shelf-building, weeding, and sweeping the dirt floor of our new house, Rusty and I have given up on taking data for the day and are listlessly hanging in the burí in the sweltering, windless heat.

Marina, the pretty young daughter of P.J. and Amelia, has just gotten married to Marcos Pala, of all people! I think she's getting the short end of the stick. Marcos Pala, an orphan, spends most of his time imitating the criollos by wearing skin-tight pants and rubbing antiperspirant on himself, and has already proven himself untrustworthy with women (his ex-wife Chitaranyí still isn't speaking to him).

Marina, on the other hand, is well trained by her mother in all aspects of cooking, sewing, weaving, child care, root-gathering, and gardening. She is young, healthy, has powerful family ties in the village, and is very pretty to boot. Right now the young couple for their honeymoon have set up a flimsy branch shelter in the mosquito-haunted woods down by the creek. Oh well . . . if Mari doesn't like this arrangement, at least she's free to change her mind.

Disease—An Interlude

FEBRUARY–APRIL 1993

In which Rusty hides our weapons;

menstruation practices; brewing manioc punch;

dysentery blues; "I'm sorry," Pumé style;

an eerie spirit creature; anyiku' tohé; Pumé

contraception; Olga; dry season metamorphosis;

Carnaval in a cowtown; Indians and Indians;

first fever; malaria nights; vampires;

mock crucifixion

2/3/93   I can now strip a little bit of go fiber, although I usually tear it badly in the process. The little girls Newe, Teresa, Olga, and Manewi are all learning how to weave too, and we spend our afternoons trotting around clutching pieces of unfinished weaving and pestering the old women. Today Teresa came over and proudly showed me her first tiny paintó, or fan; I only beat her to it by one day, and I suspect we both had a little help.

During a recent Guardia scare brought on by another low-flying plane, the Pumé all rushed out into the plaza to gawk, then turned heel and ran into their houses. Men and women yanked bows and arrows out of the roof and ran with them to the bushes outside camp, where they stashed them. This is a common Pumé response to the proximity of an enemy—we think it might be to appear less well-armed than they actually are, or to keep weapons protected. While Rusty and I watched the plane to see if it had any markings, María Florenzia came panting up to us. "Quick, hide your bows and arrows!" she whispered urgently.

Rusty obligingly took them out of our roof and scurried out to the bushes. Later, when the scare was over, he went out with everyone else to retrieve his weapons. P.J. watched him with his hands on his hips and a broad grin that as good as said, "There he goes, acting like a Pumé again . . ."

The weather has been hot and windless, about 104 degrees Fahrenheit yesterday with high humidity. All of us sat or lay wilted around camp, possessing little energy to do more than fan ourselves, complain about the heat, and pant like dogs under the cruel white sky. A few distant stormclouds tantalized us in the evening, and raised enough of a breeze to lift the paper airplanes I made for the boys—but still no rain.

Amelia, although still nursing her son Batida, started her period three days ago. All the women and girls jogged over to hear the news from her own mouth. Elbowing her way through the excited crowd, María Diachi, Amelia's mother, brought a big bunch of beautiful new red go fibers, dyed with a special leaf, which forms the women's loincloth.

Amelia, a great respecter of traditional menstruation practices, went out with her daughter Marina and gathered a big sheaf of *uringwá*, an aromatic herb that eases pains when crushed and rubbed on the body. Then Amelia got out a special set of *nyuritái*, or menstruation dishes, that no one else is allowed to use. Since no one has built a menstruation hut in this camp, she's sleeping at her parents' house in a special burí. Finally, she's not allowed to eat any fish or fishlike animals (sting rays, eels, turtles, and so on) for the duration of her period.

All this commotion has apparently inspired my own body, and now I'm menstruating too. As I write, Doña Carmen, Marina, Amelia, and I are *nyurí*, and fish is off-limits to all of us. It's a good thing Trino went out after a deer, and P.J. is hunting for birds. Yona only just stopped, and María Luisa is about due to start. It's getting as bad as a college dorm out here.

2/5/93   I've made my first batch of bai eró, or fermented manioc punch. Here's the recipe:

Ingredients
1 big gourdful of water
2 large, fresh tambái cakes
1 woman with nothing more pressing to do

Directions
Only women's spit is supposed to work (men have to scare up a female relative to help). Take a small bite out of the first tambái and chew it for about a minute, or until you can taste the starch beginning to sweeten in your mouth (just as Saltine crackers do). Spit the mouthful of tambái into the water. Take another bite, chew carefully, and spit; repeat until

all the tambái has been processed. On a hot day you'll need several gulps of water to help you salivate.

Cover the gourd with a cloth and tie a string around the mouth to keep bugs out. Put up out of kids' reach and leave for about 12–14 hours. The longer you let it sit, the more alcoholic it gets. When ready, it should be slightly foamy. A really good batch is sweet and tangy, with a little alcoholic bite like a light beer.

All Pumé, including kids, love this stuff, and after my initial reluctance last winter, I, too, became addicted. It's usually served as a refreshment during and after tohé, but sometimes women just make a batch because they're in the mood. Without chewing, this punch would be impossible, as it's the saliva that breaks the starches down into sugars, which then ferment.

One of Rusty's colleagues spent a year working with the Piro people in Peru, who have made this punch the center of their social life; they let it sit three days until it's good and hard, then have big drunken parties that end when the last person falls over in a stupor.

2/6/93   Late last night I awoke abruptly from a sound sleep with horrible pangs in my belly. I quickly burrowed out from underneath the hii, or mosquito net, and trotted through the dim moonlight to the bushes with not a second to spare. Diarrhea out here involves the usual miseries, plus mosquito bites all over your butt and mosquitoes inside the hii biting you for the rest of the night because you've broken the seal. I writhed myself into a tortured sleep only to have to run out again two hours later, and again at dawn. We've decided I have a light case of amoebic dysentery, and I've been walloping it with powerful drugs. I feel a little better now, but totally exhausted.

I managed to dredge up some appetite when Francisco and Eulogio returned laden with food from a trading trip. Today is Rusty's birthday, and I was able to cook and share his birthday feast. The menu:

Rabbit Soup
Butcher one adult rabbit and be sure to rinse the sand off the pieces. Add water to cover and boil over a moderate fire for about ten minutes. Salt to taste, and remove pieces when tender and white all the way through. Set meat aside (out of reach of dogs and kids) to cool, and leave broth in the pot on the fire.

Stewed Turtle Eggs
Remove shreds of turtle uterus from eggs and add shreds to the rabbit broth. Carefully tear leathery shell off eggs and

shake gently until yolks and whites fall into the broth. Boil till yolks are slightly firm; remove eggs and meat and eat quickly while still warm. Leave broth on the fire.

Turtle Soup
Butcher your share of the turtle (in our case, strip muscle from foreleg bone, leaving fatty paw intact, and pick liver, heart, kidneys and lungs apart). Boil pieces well in broth until tender, about 15 minutes. Remove meat and set aside with rabbit to cool. Snack on these pieces and feed them to your dinner guest if he's getting impatient.

Multi-Species Rice Stew
Pour raw rice into super-rich (rabbit, egg, turtle) broth and cook over low fire until goopy. Salt to taste. Serve hot.

Roast Cayman Tail
Cut tail lengthwise and remove vertebrae, which should come out all connected together. Roast "butterflied" tail on both sides until meat is white and a little browned at the edges. Set carefully aside for tomorrow, since you're both too gorged to eat another bite.

2/7/93   Everyone is in a funny mood today. With the cash a few of the men had earned working for the ranchers, Marcos Pala walked to the ranch and bought two bottles of *caño blanco*, the "Everclear" of the llanos. Nearly everyone took a few sips, and P.J. began to orate and gesticulate energetically. A couple of boys came running, saying that young Juan Masano had just passed out in the bushes.

Rusty and I went over to have a look after he'd been carried back into camp. We assumed it was the alcohol, but as Dos Pasos

propped Juan up in a sitting position we noticed that his handsome, dark face was slack, the eyes open and rolled back to show
the whites. His mouth hung open and long strings of saliva trailed
onto his shirt, giving him a weird, drugged look. Everyone acted
puzzled and asked each other what he had eaten. Juan stayed unconscious for over half an hour while people attempted to feed
him sugar water and wipe water in his hair and on his face. While
excited kids scampered around them, old Dos Pasos sang, blew in
Juan's ear, and pulled briskly on his limp fingers to crack the
knuckles.

Strangely, during all the commotion Juan's wife María Llovina
showed no concern or sympathy. Just after he came out of his
faint, she walked to their house and is now busily going through
all their belongings. Some of Juan's things are in a pile at the edge
of camp, others are being tossed either into the trash heap or into
a bonfire María has built. It sure looks like another divorce to me,
and I hate to see this happy marriage go on the rocks.

2/13/93   María Florenzia and I lie a few meters apart in our respective hammocks in our respective houses, she with her drowsy
baby, I with my dog-eared journal. It's a hot windy afternoon with
lots of flies. Nearly everyone is asleep after tohé last night, although I can hear muted conversation in P.J.'s house (if only one
house in camp ever has talk going on, it's P.J.'s).

The only other sounds are the lazy buzz of fat flies and the occasional growled, "*Hatchí!*" or, "Get outta here!" from me or María
Florenzia, directed at the panting, tick-ridden dogs trying to lie
in the shade of our houses. As I write, I can hear the happy ech-
oes of shouts and laughter floating up from the creek; the kids
are playing there to escape the doldrums of a campful of sleepy
grownups.

María Llovina and Juan Masano seem to have patched up their
quarrel of a few days ago. The way we interpret the gossip, the day

they had the fight Juan felt so terrible that he wandered out into the woods and ate a special plant. The plant, which brought on his strange fit, seems to be a means of showing regret; the Pumé have no words we know of to say, "I'm sorry." Until I can get a name and a specimen for my collection, I'm going to call it the regret plant.

My weakness and nausea are clinging stubbornly to me, and I have the classic bloody, mucus-covered stool of amoebic dysentery. I've been eating the horribly bitter medicine for a week, but it doesn't seem to be helping. There is a definite tenderness in my right side, and we're guessing the amoebas are encysting in my liver. We're not sure what to do now; I haven't eaten anything substantial since the 7th, and am very slow to notice and understand things.

I've noticed that the Pumé, even when they are really sick, don't seem to think about death very much, unless it's imminent. When a death occurs, people weep and wail openly for a few days, then settle into quiet reminiscence. Prolonged depression over death doesn't seem to exist, although sometimes the women will cry for a few minutes, thinking about a family member long dead.

Real morbidity must be a city luxury, where death is kept out of sight and smell in hospitals and mortuaries, or portrayed artily in books, paintings, and movies. Out here, death is all around us, always in our faces. Why obsess about it when so many more interesting things are happening?

Last night there was no dance, and everyone was lying sleepily in their houses in the fragrant darkness of a dry season night. Suddenly a strange noise came floating up to us from the south; first distantly, then clearly, we heard *"Pdeek! Pdeek! Pdeek!"* as some flying creature approached. It sounded unearthly, a high, bloodless cry unlike any insect, bat, or bird I've ever heard before. The creature circled camp once, flew off to the west, returned and circled again, then flew away to the north, crying the whole time.

At its first approach, the Pumé were silent, listening intently. Then Lucrecia called to her son P.J. and he began to talk loudly to the creature, calling it *hiámui*, or mother's father. Lucrecia and her big brother Dos Pasos began to orate to the creature and continued long after it had flown away.

The Pumé also address the huge, ghostly barn owls of the llanos as ancestors, but the encounter with this creature was more eerie because I couldn't connect its voice with any sound I knew. The Pumé were truly unnerved by it, and we knew it had visited Rufina's camp because her thin, piercing voice floated over to us on the breeze for the rest of the night.

I would never have thought that her voice (normally a quavering half-whisper) could be capable of such strength and clarity. The only time women sing solo is when they are inspired in the night, in the solitude of their hammocks. Their song is called *anyikui tohé*, or the little sister ceremony, and an older woman of spiritual power will sing alone all night long. I can picture Rufina, tiny, wrinkled and blind, lying there in her burí in the darkness, sending a spreading cone of song into the night sky for all the unquiet Old Ones who fly, hoot, and squeak; and for Kumanyí, the goddess who created all things living, dead and in-between.

When I visited criolla Lu's house the next morning, she talked excitedly about the mysterious creature, which had also flown over her family's house. "We heard it squeaking and flying over our heads—it must have been really big!" she whispered to me. "We were scared!" She agrees with the Pumé that it is no earthly bird or animal, but a supernatural being. I guess I'll never know what it was.

We've finally decided, after much debate, to go to town to see if I can get over this illness. I haven't been able to take data for two weeks, and was so weak hiking to the ranch that I got heat exhaustion, then terrible shivers when I tried to bathe. A tiny scratch will bleed copiously for minutes. I feel miserable and am unsuccessfully fighting off attacks of guilt to be disrupting the project like this.

The ranchers are openly astonished at my refusal of their rich cooking. They're used to watching us unashamedly scarfing down everything on the table that isn't on someone else's plate, and my loss of appetite has convinced them that I must be really good and sick.

2/17/93   After a gruelling truck ride we're in town now, in our favorite little hotel with marble floors and strange old Italian furniture and drapes covered with red velvet curlicues. As I lie in bed, choke down pills, and drink soup, I float back and forth in my mind, seeking memories of Doro Aná I haven't yet had the time to record.

Just before we left camp, I had a frank talk with Amelia about Pumé women's birth control. She said Dori, María Luisa, and Gusha, all in their childbearing prime, have chosen not to have babies because they are frightened of the risks of childbirth. Amelia says the way women keep from getting pregnant is eating a plant that she calls *uin déh toh*. In all my time here I have not heard of an unwanted pregnancy, and I would judge this plant to be reasonably effective. There is also an abortifacient plant called *uin chiá toh* that you can take up until three months of gestation have passed. As with all such remedies, Amelia says it's a dangerous poison and is very painful to use.

I got out my birth control pills and showed them to her, joking about how expensive they are and how she should show me where the uin déh toh grows. She laughed but made no offers, and I'm guessing it's a valuable resource the Pumé women don't want me plundering with my plant-pressing kit.

Later in the day Amelia brought her little sister Docharanyí over to see my birth control pills. I explained to them that I too am frightened of childbirth, and this explanation has since percolated through camp. The questions regarding my being pregnant or not have stopped; it's now understood that I've chosen not to conceive for the time being, and have the means to prevent it.

All my adult life I've clung to the faith that women in all times and places, whether overtly or in secret, will find the means to control their reproduction. This small confirmation from the Pumé, who treat the matter as a woman's own business, is a good and solid thing. I feel as though I've reached out in the dark behind me and felt another woman's hand.

2/16/93   In a reverie today I thought about Olga, one of my favorite little girls. About six years old, she is the middle daughter of María Florenzia and Francisco. Her name is pronounced "Orga" since the Pumé have no "l" sound. Olga has a big, round comical face whose front teeth just came in—her profile is a little horsey, like her mother's. She has a stocky little girl's body set on surprisingly long, slender legs that, on the rare occasions that she's naked, make her look like a water tower. Her voice is unusually deep and rich and easily distinguishable from the other girls', especially her laugh, which is bouncy and contagious.

Olga is one of the most popular playmates in camp, always good-natured, creative, and daring, and when she is away visiting with her family the girls left behind in camp will sing during their games: "*Oru-ga, manawú, Oru-ga, manawú . . .* " ("Olga, come back, Olga, come back . . ."). Like most middle children, Olga has a complicated relationship with her mother, and when she's angry at María Florenzia she indulges in spectacular crying fits that last for hours, taking on a doped, mechanical quality and driving all of us insane. But these fits are getting less frequent as she gets older.

The day we left for town I was lying in the burí zoning out when she came over, climbed onto our chair, and began her favorite game. Olga, like all the girls, is really interested in Rusty's daughter back home, who is also considered to be my daughter, although she has a different mother. So the game always begins with Olga asking, *"Na habí, na ta kéhinyi?"* ("Your daughter, what's her name?") My answer: *"Claudia kéhinyi!"* And then Olga: *"Craudia kéhinyi!"* and a big smile.

She'll ask me this five times a day if she's in the mood, so today I astonished her by taking the offensive: *"Adóh na habí, na ta kéhinyi?"* She blushed and squirmed, managing to giggle out that she doesn't yet have a daughter. I acted surprised. *"Oideh ka?"* I asked. More giggles—no, no husband, either. But she recovered nicely and pointed at little Newe, who'd joined us, and said, *"Bomái!"* I peered at Newe's belly skeptically and announced that she sure didn't look pregnant to me.

After some more joking the girls decided the occasion called for energetic play-wrestling under my burí, which Manewi ran in from the plaza to join. I almost never remember to write down these little exchanges that Rusty and I have, usually several times a day, with the kids, but they are one of the best features of our life out here.

2/17/93   Some of my most tranquil reminiscences are of trips with the old women. A few weeks ago I went out with Lucrecia and Diacricia to gather yipái. As usual, we started early, walking east across the grass with thin bright sunlight in our eyes and a cold wind in our faces. Both old women were equipped with toréh (the slender-bladed digging shovels), enormous taiyó baskets, and assorted lengths of string.

We stopped a few times on the near side of the creek to search for yipái roots—it's a whole new ball game in the dry season, now that the yipái leaves and stems are dead. They are brown and crisped and look exactly like all the other millions of drying grass stems. I had just begun to pride myself on being able to spot yipái in the wet season, but now if I manage to spot two tiny, shriveled stalks in a whole day's trip I count myself lucky. The old women, of course, are experts at it—they part the grass with their digging tools and peer carefully (reminding me of parting someone's hair to search for nits).

After finding very little, we crossed the doró, using a tiny winding trail through the dense growth of trees and vines that grown on the banks. It's like going through a tunnel; the plants seem to hang over you, watching as you scuttle underneath, trying carefully to brush aside the terrible razor grass. We collected a few leaves of baby moriche palm to be processed for weaving, and came out of the creek bed to a favorite yipái-picking spot. Both grandmas began digging steadily along a promising belt.

Part of my data collection involves tallying how many roots the women pick per minute, and I noticed that they were only picking about half as quickly as in the wet season, when the stalks are obvious. But their patience is enormous and implacable. Empty bellies at home and there's no turning back until the taiyó are full. The way old Pumé women dig roots is almost like a natural force, like wind or water wearing away at a coastline—steady, inexorable, and without visible exertion. I know this isn't true; it's damn tiring work for them, but watching them is truly hypnotizing.

Diacricia told me to go hang out in the shade, since they were going to be at it for a long while. "Go sit over there," she joked, pointing to a nice shade tree, "and write whatever it is that you write. Write it down!"

I laughed with her and moved off toward the tree, then nearly fell over backward when I stepped on the tail of a young brocket deer and it exploded out from underneath me. The grandmas whooped and the deer bounded away, bright rust-red against the trees. We sorrowfully watched it vanish from sight, our bellies growling.

Several hours of picking later, we walked back west into the doró bed and stopped at a tiny pond to rinse our mud-covered roots. We heard boys yelling in the distance and the grandmas told me to whisper—they didn't want any criollos to know where we were. We washed the roots in silence, broken only once by a loud fart from Lucrecia that sent us all into stifled giggles.

After reloading the clean yipái and putting the heavy taiyó on their heads (my little sidepack, full of roots, was also on my head), we came out on the west side of the creek to find that a gang of Pumé boys from our camp had just chopped down a tree to get a honeycomb. True to their nature, they had begun to devour the honey on-site, without any intention of bringing any home. When we marched up, they shamefacedly gave each of us a handful of honeycomb and we mashed it into our faces. None of us had eaten in more than twenty-four hours, and the wild, fragrant sweetness filled our parched mouths with a shocking pleasure that shone in the eyes of the old women as though they were little girls.

Now pleasantly sticky, we took our leave of the boys and walked northwest to an area that was poor in yipái, but we did come across a fresh arí (cayman) butchering and roasting spot. The grandmas were absolutely furious; they could tell that the arí had been butchered and parts of it eaten clandestinely, instead of being taken home whole to be shared out to the hungry women and children in camp. We later found out it was Dionso, who had as usual stuffed himself in the field before bringing home the leftovers.

Still grumbling, we searched unsuccessfully for more roots, then worked our way over to a nice stand of baby palm trees. The old women dropped their heavy taiyós and spread out, searching for the young palm leaves and chopping the stems with their toréh blades. Diacricia, aware that I am trying to learn how to weave, kindly pointed out a few bunches for me to pick for myself. The grandmas then began chopping mature leaves with which to patch their house roofs.

Lucrecia went to work on a big young tree, stacking the leaves as she chopped them off. She then attacked the trunk, peeling and chopping and peeling until she'd exposed the clean ivory-white heart of the palm. With more skillful chopping she freed up several crisp, sweet chunks of palm heart about the size of a woman's forearm.

After handing me most of it (grandmas are always mindful of the voracious appetites of us young women), she pushed a few chunks into her own mouth, called her co-wife over, and gave her the rest. Both grandmas munched while they rearranged their prodigious loads of yipái and tied on the palm leaf bundles. Lucrecia had so much that I had to help her load up—she looked like a couple of baskets with leaves stacked on top, with a pair of thin brown legs sticking out underneath. She would have carried the heavy toréh too, but I offered to lug it home for her and she accepted with a smile.

Bent nearly double under their loads, they trotted off down the trail in the ferocious two o'clock heat. We made it home about forty minutes later, where hungry families, firewood-gathering, and cooking were waiting for us. A few chuckles from the younger women (who know better than to follow their mothers on these marathon trips) greeted me as I dragged myself into camp. The boiled roots felt good in my belly, and with the small bobuí leaves I'd collected I wove my first paintó fan.

2/17/93   The heat of the summer squeezes the llanos like a giant fist, draining the creeks, lowering the rivers, and leaving small ponds isolated in the drying landscape. The fish, crowded together, are feeding on plants and each other, getting fat in anticipation of the synchronized May spawning. As the oxygen level drops in the stagnating water, the fish have begun to jump out to gulp air, which they store in special sacs. This activity makes them easy prey for the birds, who have settled in for the season and whose weird calls fill the air day and night.

The Pumé usually go after fish and birds at dawn and dusk, and this part of the year persistent hunters like Gonzalo can bag enough game to be able to share out and still have plenty left over for the family cookpot. Water-loving animals like turtles, caymans, and capybara are concentrating around shrinking wet areas, and the river Pumé are busy hunting them. Whether our area has been overhunted or the habitat isn't wet enough, we are seeing very few of these larger animals except through trade with the river Pumé.

The drying landscape has withered the stalks and leaves of many of the food roots like yipái, chokuí, and pará. Sometimes the women comb the grasses meticulously for telltale dried stalks (as on my recent trip with the two grandmas). Other times the women go to an area they already know has roots, and sit down and tirelessly mine for them with their digging tools.

Since yipái grows as scattered individual plants, the combing strategy is most successful; pará, which grows in concentrated "veins," can be found by sifting through the dirt generated by digging long trenches. Soon the mangos will come into season and groups of men and women will set out on long journeys to the river's edge where the best trees grow.

The days begin cool and windy, and the sun gets fierce around noon and stays that way until just before it sets. Even the oblique sunlight of the early evening is too hot to sit in. The nights, though, are blessedly cool with little breezes that scurry through blankets and keep the mosquitoes down. All in all, the dry season is beautiful, much kinder to human beings than the wet season, and I'm sorry to be sick and indoors during such a pleasant time of year.

2/19/93 One aspect of the summer I'm not so fond of is the increased alcohol consumption that accompanies the seasonal travel and wage work on the ranches. The savanna Pumé generally treat alcohol like they would any other drug; when they've got it, they hit it hard. Drunkenness is called niwí, the same term they use for the nanú-inspired hallucinations, and is treated with respect.

Since the Doro Aná Pumé have almost no access to cash, the alcohol supply is scanty and irregular. Although Rusty and I put on our disapproving faces whenever bottles of the stuff show up (too many horrible memories of drunk Navajo men and women sprawled along the Gallup, New Mexico, roadside), we can't yet see alcohol causing much damage in Doro Aná. But in river communities like Chenchenita there are many alcoholic Pumé, and the faces of our savanna friends and family contort with fear and distaste when they discuss the latest drunken brawls on the river.

2/23/93   Back to the present: it's time again for Carnaval, the wild festival that precedes Holy Week, and the little cowtown of San Fernando is rising enthusiastically to the occasion. It's customary to toss buckets full of water at strangers, and we've been drenched by happy kids throwing water out of passing cars or overhead windows, yelling "*Agua carajo!*" Colorful streamers, tissue paper flowers, masks, and piñatas adorn the houses and streetlights, and everyone is running around in silly costumes.

This evening while we were fighting our way through a rowdy crowd on the main street, a young man in flamboyant drag (including watermelon breasts and a pregnant belly) teetered up to Rusty on his high heels and smooched pink lipstick all over him, cooing, "Ay, *mi guapito, ven con migo* . . ."

All the little kids are dressed up as they would be in the big city, but the costumes are homemade and a lot more original. One of my favorites, which is very popular this year, is the North American Plains Indian costume complete with fringed buckskin, warpaint, and feathers, or braids and leather jumpers for the little girls. All this, when the Pumé are right next door! Gemma once told us that in a river Pumé schoolhouse there's a criollo painting of one of those Plains warriors on a horse, wearing a full warbonnet. The confused Pumé kids take the feathers of his headdress to be wildly colorful, bristling locks of hair.

2/25/93   We are spending money like water, but I still have chest and head pain, and the other night I had a frightening fever that kept me delirious for hours while poor Rusty tried to keep wet towels on me. But I'm really missing the Pumé. I just want to hang around and talk with them, to see familiar, comfortable things like María Florenzia washing her baby, or María Diachi hiking up her skirt to scratch her butt, or P.J. and Rusty sharing a cigar at our hearth.

Sometimes at night, when people are settled down to sleep, P.J. likes to call over to Rusty. It's just like girl scout camp, or a slumber party. "*Aji? Ajimúi? Ajimúi! Ajimúi?*" ("Big brother . . . ?") he'll call over and over again. Half the time I have to shake Rusty out of a deep sleep so he can answer.

Other times we've been busy with other matters, and I remember clearly two instances when the Pumé have caught us fooling around, as we thought, secretly. Once María Llovina called loudly over to me, "Are you sleeping?" I decorously answered, "Yes, I'm, uh, sleeping." There followed a chorus of stifled laughter and María said, "Oh, is that so?" with rich sarcasm. Another time I forgot myself and gasped, and from across camp we heard P.J. give a perfect imitation of it, to appreciative giggles. If you learn one thing living with the Pumé, it's not to take yourself very seriously.

3/13/93   By March 10th I was feeling weak but restless, and both of us decided to go back to Doro Aná. So we made the long truck ride back to Hato San Jacinto, which took two days because of a big storm. When we jumped off the truck I was exhausted from the trip and felt feverish, but dismissed it as a common cold that had been going around town.

The next morning the fever soared and I've had a hellish few

days, during which I've been delirious about half the time. A repeating sequence of fever, chills, and pouring sweats assault me,
with crippling head and body pains like I'm being stretched on
the rack. Any change in altitude, as when I try to get out of the
hammock to pee, fills my eyes with tears from the pain. Moraima
and Paco, with understanding smiles, both say I've got *paludismo*,
the criollo word for malaria.

After poor Rusty had jogged back to Doro Aná, checked the
medicine book, and chatted with the Pumé, he agrees with the
ranchers. So in a few more days we'll hitch *another* ride into town,
and I'm trying not to panic from fear of the disease and from our
lack of money. If I think about how much time this is taking away
from the project, I want to scream. But I can't do anything about
it, and I have to let others make my decisions for me now.

One of the criolla nostrums young Moraima has kindly offered
me is *manteca de caiman*, or crocodile fat—a sweet, oily table-
spoonful. One morning she also gave me a teacup full of lemon
juice and sugar slowly heated together into a delicious, soothing
syrup. Although I've enjoyed the remedies, they haven't really
had much effect other than to increase my affection for Moraima.
For the last few days she and her lively toddler Amanda have been
keeping me company as I lie limply in my hammock on the porch.

3/15/93   During my worst night I had no concept of the passage
of time, although I was vaguely aware of Rusty sitting in a chair
next to me, swinging me in the hammock, and fanning me to keep
the fever from climbing. Our little thermometer hovered between
104 and 105 degrees Fahrenheit. Rusty tried to sponge me with
cool water that felt like searing acid to my burning skin, and I
writhed away, fighting him with weak slaps. Sometimes I lapsed
into vivid hallucinations, and he and the hot, dark little room disappeared.

A tall woman with a strange, triangular, mantislike face stood on a hill in front of me. Her eyes were very dark, pupilless, and radiant with sympathy. She wore a long white dress that covered her feet and hands, and on her head she carried a huge earthen pot, much like the ones the river Pumé still make. Somehow I knew its contents would help me. But before I could ask her to help me she disappeared.

Abruptly my lungs turned into twin burning towers. At the summit of each stood a young white man in a business suit. They pointed to the different parts of my body that were in pain: my head, spine, joints, lungs, stomach. They explained to me that for each pain I was paying for a similar pain I'd inflicted on someone in the past. It took all night for them to go over each part of my body. I couldn't move or cry, and I really thought I might die or lose my mind in those endless hours. If Rusty hadn't been near me I don't know what might have happened.

We spent two more days at the ranch and yesterday drove back into town. We went to the malaria clinic today and I tested positive for falciparum malaria, the kind that has the highest fatality rate if left untreated. The agonizing pains in my head are from the plasmodium organisms causing punctate hemorrhages in my brain.

I've now taken the treatment and will return to the clinic for a follow-up in case there are any plasmodia lodged in my liver. I'm keeping my red blood cells crossed. I'm still wobbly at the knees, weak, and apt to cry at odd moments. But I'm grateful, to belly-crawling abjectness, not to have to undergo another paroxysm.

3/20/93   We were chatting yesterday with one of the rare North Americans in San Fernando, a young Mormon missionary. He said an old grandmother recently pleaded with him not to kidnap and murder her grandchildren. She had obviously mistaken the missionary for a member of a vampirelike group of entrepreneurs called *pixtecas*, notorious throughout South America for stealing children.

The Venezuelans believe that the pixtecas are in league with the Cubans. Kidnapped children are drugged or murdered and their eyes and large quantities of blood removed. The Venezuelans claim that the Cubans then use the eyes and blood to revitalize the fiendish Fidel Castro, whose aging, decrepit body supposedly consumes large quantities of hijacked organs every year.

Although my first impulse was to smile at this ghoulish semilegend, I know there is a desperate need for donated organs, which fetch high prices, in most countries. South American children periodically turn up in third world back alleys with odd injuries, and white tourists have had close brushes with angry mobs in recent years. One woman from Colorado was actually killed by a mob in Guatemala several years ago after she was seen talking to a small boy and he subsequently disappeared.

By contrast, Rusty and I have become the pet foreigners in this little town. People in the streets, or our favorite bakeries, shops, and restaurants, yell out a cheerful greeting whenever we walk in.

3/23/93   We keep bumping into a frightening priest who seems to travel around quite a bit; we've seen him here and in the frontier town of La Lechuga during the strike in October, when he was surrounded by the angry crowd at La Lechuga's ferry-crossing.

Around six feet tall and maybe four hundred pounds, his skin is brilliant red, like a pastrami. His tiny silver spectacles cling to his face like a spider despite the sweat washing down, and wispy long hair, the yellow of dirty ivory, adorns his shiny pink scalp. He wears an enormous white tentlike cassock from chin to toe, and a heavy silver cross on a chain hangs down the curving expanse of his belly. Whenever I see him in the midst of his wiry brown parishioners he reminds me of a huge, bloated white palm grub in a swarm of ants.

The other day we saw him struggling into a tiny red car outside a bakery, like Moby Dick trying to submerge into a shoebox. It doesn't make me feel any friendlier toward him to think of the evangelized Pumé in the river communities, who are now forbidden to hold tohé or practice other traditional rites. Tohé-less Pumé would be like blind, mute birds with clipped wings; I want to cry thinking of the children who will never know the tohé ceremony.

I understand that the adult Pumé in evangelized communities simply go and visit other villages when they're in the mood for a dance, but their children are being taught by the evangelists that the creatoress Kumanyí and all the Pumé spirits and deities are evil demons. For these children and their children it's already too late.

It is *Semana Santa*, or Holy Week, and the mock-crucifixions have begun across South America and in the Philippines. Men and women are actually nailed to crosses after their hands and feet are tied to the beams. The martyrs are then raised up to hang in tormented piety for hours or even days. The churches are crammed with worshippers and there are ornate processions in the streets daily.

I look around at all the hoopla and feel utterly bewildered. Pumé writhing around zonkered on nanú, or dancing around a pole all night, look pretty sensible next to a mock crucifixion. I can imagine the blank look of a Pumé confronted with such a spectacle—in this, I feel a sense of unity with the Indians; in this, I am closer to them than I am to the modern Catholic.

We Mark Our First Year Here, Dry Season to Wet Season

APRIL–MAY 1993

In which we return to Doro Aná; the death

of a son; Lu's ordeal; new Pumé on the way;

the wet season move; mangos in the sunset;

"tohé ngwá!"; a dog's life; water; Diacricia's face;

evils of wage work; chinakarú in the pot;

mantis-baiting; a terrible beating; the oldest Pumé;

stork-hunting jokes; boa in the grass;

Rufina on the edge

4/19/93   At long last we set out of town Saturday afternoon in good criollo style: three hours late, in the back of a truck perched on a mountain of baggage, clutching huge plastic cups of cheap whiskey cut with a splash of orange Gatorade (I've christened this the Llanos Cocktail). After a hellish long ride we reached the Pumé community of Chenchenita in the middle of the night. Through my haze of exhaustion I could hear the women's chorus coming from the tohé ceremony nearby, floating out to us through the rainy darkness like a fierce welcome.

This morning at the ranch while we were waiting for a truck ride to camp, who should come parading in but P.J. and a big gang of women and girls with taiyó baskets, looking for mangos. What they got instead were their two pet niwéi, a bunch of pasta and rice, and a scary ride home on the back of a wildly bouncing truck. My little sister Dori stuck close to me the whole time, and was the first to tell me that her one-year-old nephew, José Ahi, had died four days before.

When we got back and were sharing out the food, the baby's mother María Romero and her family came over from their little camp. She told me quietly that her son was dead, and I, who don't know how to say I'm sorry in Pumé, told her I'd been too far away to be able to help. The other women murmured in agreement; they weren't accusing about it, they were just saying what is true. María Romero pointed up to the beautiful blue sky and told me her boy is now up there, in Kumanyí's country.

José Ahi died on a dark, rainy Thursday. He was a big, strong boy, just learning to walk, whom I'd secretly named Buddha because of his bald head, fat belly, and wise face. He looked a lot like his wild big sister Micheda, who was his main caretaker. He was always shy of us, never smiling when he was in our house. This is my second death here, and the first of someone I knew well. All I could do while María Romero stood next to me, her eyes streaming with tears, was cry along with her, cry for them both.

I try to turn my attention to the living now. There have been some changes in the many days we've been gone; little Ana is very strong now, and yells with lots of character like the big girl she is. She peed all over me to welcome me home. Docharanyí had waited till I was gone to give birth in March to a very big baby girl with beautiful thick hair and a big, healthy squawking voice.

Juana Trina, whose baby girl we brought through that terrible illness last July, has left her husband (who had taken up with another woman) and come to live with Rufina. It's worrisome to have Juana Trina and her three girls, and Chitaranyí and *her* two children without husbands to help them survive the coming wet season. Some Pumé men have a pretty poor batting average with sticking by the families they help start. Luckily, women here have lots of family nearby to cushion the hardship of breakups. I guess Pumé women are more fortunate than many in the world. Still, it makes me wonder, were human males meant by nature to help with offspring? Or are the men who stay and help raise the children exceptions to the rule?

Rusty says the Doro Aná women are really glad to see me after our long separation. I wasn't sure at first—people are always pretty casual about comings and goings here—but the women and their children have now been continuously in our house, with a short break last night for sleep, for well over twenty-four hours. Right now I'm laying on the tabadá and little Batida is sitting next to me with one hand on me and the other on the notebook, watching with interest as I write. His mother Amelia is sitting next to us grooming the thick, glossy hair of Gusha, who is lying in her lap.

Little Domana is cruising for a bruising, pushing babies around and making them cry. Doña Carmen is sitting in the chair carving a pretty silver bracelet for herself out of a beer can with a small knife. Dori is sitting quietly, catlike, in another chair. It's very hot and humid with almost no wind. Even the Pumé women sitting around me are glistening with sweat, tiny silver beads on their brown upper lips. We are all hungry and the women have been teasing the baby boys all day: "Hey, go catch us some fish!"

4/21/93 Yesterday during a hot, quiet afternoon our criolla neighbor Lu and her boys dropped on our camp like a bomb. During a quarrel with her husband Daniel, he'd picked up a heavy stick and beat her and the eldest boy. Lu, crying and shaking, showed the excited Pumé her ugly welts, which included the hand wounds characteristic of attempted self-defense.

She told us she was going to La Paz, a tiny town to the northeast of us. All she'd brought were a gotaiyó bag filled with a few clothes, some Kotex, a baby bottle, and a hammock. She had no food, water, money, or family to turn to. Rusty filled up a spare bottle with water and gave her some aspirins against the hot sun. We had not a cent we could give her.

She set off for a small farm about five miles away, carrying the baby and trailed by her two little boys. She seemed so despondent I decided to walk with her part-way, at least. Rusty ran after us with more water, a hat, and sunscreen—fortunately, because as it turned out I decided to walk the whole way with them. It seemed like a hell of a long way carrying the baby, and her biggest boy Angelito wasn't strong enough to carry the bag with all their goods.

Finally, I went along because Lu seemed so downcast; since she has no family, she said she would have to throw herself on the charity of the National Guard soldier outpost. The options for criolla women on the run with no family to fall back on are almost nonexistent.

We walked, with frequent pauses for rest, sips of water, and to smear on sunscreen, for about three hours in the blazing, merciless sun of the equatorial summer. Lu and Angelito, the eldest son, were barefoot. Angelito is about seven years old and the younger boy about four, but they toughed it out; they're criollo boys.

During a break under the scanty shade of a small tree, curly-haired Angelito, who is always cheerful and alert, glanced at me and asked his mother, "These two have a lot of heart, don't they?" Lu said yes in a low voice, avoiding my eyes. When I thought about the boy, walking in the hot sun with a back swollen from the beating and no food in his belly, I felt like crying.

We got to the farm in the late afternoon, the boys very tired but in good spirits, and the baby amazingly perky and cheerful. Lu told the family there about the situation, and I was unpleasantly surprised to see them laugh and shrug. After kissing Lu goodbye, I borrowed a bicycle to pedal to Hato San Jacinto, and struggled along the sandy road in the slanting evening sunshine. I passed several Doro Aná Pumé men working in the ranchers' field, and they straightened up with astonished grins as I pedaled gamely past.

When I reached Hato San Jacinto I chatted briefly with Moraima, who was watching the store, and Fernando, one of Moleto's boys. Lu's plight met with no sympathy there, either. Moraima said Lu must be crazy to run off with no money and three kids, and Fernando informed us that "it must be her own fault, because if a woman behaves herself her husband doesn't need to beat her." As Fernando is notorious for his own wife-beating habits, I bit my tongue and set off for Doro Aná on foot.

Being very tired I wove back and forth, constantly changing my mind about which trail was best. I had hiked and biked about thirteen miles since the beginning of the afternoon. Rusty met me on the big hill outside of camp and we walked home together.

Of course, the Pumé were dying with curiosity when we got home. P.J. had already talked with Daniel and gave a half-hearted defense of his behavior, claiming that Lu is *chuanyí*, or ferocious. But although the women are amused (niwéi squabbles are comical to them), they're not fooled. No woman has been struck or even yelled at in Doro Aná in all our time here. I'm tired, and angry at Lu's unsympathetic neighbors, especially the women. I wonder if I'll ever see her again.

Gusha is pregnant! I asked her how far along, and she said about three months. She, along with teenaged Carmen Cartoria, can expect to give birth within weeks of each other. I'm excited for Gusha—as far as we know, this is her first. Her pregnancy has really brought her out of her shell; she's much more social, tending everyone's babies and joining the women in their mass visits to my house. She is now an unfamiliar, quiet presence in the corner, following the conversation and smiling to herself.

Despite the recent rains and humidity, the water level is staying low. Our bathing pool, which was chest-high when we left for town, is now barely hip-high and scummy. The new young plants' bright greenery, brought on by early rains, looks funny next to the shallow creek. There are baby chokuí shoots everywhere—Amelia dug up four of them sprouting under our shelf the other day. The wet season may have its bad points, but my mouth waters at the thought of the little white chokuí roots winking up like pearls from the dark, upturned earth.

4/22/93   In the last two days we've gotten two arí, or caymans, one about five feet long and the other over six feet long. They were both males and we got no bonus of eggs or young with them, but they were fat with dry season fish and tasted delicious.

Rusty, who was on one of the hunts yesterday, said the Pumé had located the animal's burrow in the creek bank a day earlier. The men had to dig for hours while the trapped cayman gulped and growled fiercely, especially when the men probed into the hole with an arrow. Finally, they plunged one of the big arí harpoons into him and dragged him fighting into the open, and shot five arrows quickly into his head to blind him. Then they chopped at his neck and the base of his tail with machetes to sever the spinal cord.

These reptiles really have a lot of fight in them—an hour later P.J. gave me a big piece of the tail column and it writhed in my hands while I tried to cut it into stew-sized chunks. It reminded me of a turtle we once saw killed and butchered; when it was nothing more than a pile of bloody meat, the little teardrop-shaped heart went on stubbornly beating for several minutes.

Today Rusty and I spent the afternoon rummaging through the houses in the empty wet season camp, doing an interesting inventory on what kinds of things the Pumé leave behind during their stay in other camps. Aside from the trash, they commonly store items for later retrieval and use, such as arrows, mortars, and small odds-and-ends like string, old baskets, and bits of cloth, which they tuck in the roofs of the houses for safety.

I remember hiking up there last April to have a look around, and what a wasteland it seemed. An empty Pumé camp has a rumpled, exhausted look to it: all bleached bones, brittle scraps of thrice-used cloth, and shreds of woven artifacts peeping wearily up from dusty trash piles like fossils from another era. The wind-scoured sand and weeds and the partly caved-in houses add to the sense of desolation.

It forcibly reminded me how far away an archaeological site is from the yelling, crying, laughing, singing, farting reality of the people who lived there. Those who are attracted to the seeming loneliness and sadness of old sites love the ashes without remembering the light and warmth of the fire.

4/23/93   This morning we all moved back to our wet season camp, the one we'd explored yesterday, about three-quarters of a mile away, on higher ground. Unlike other moves, where the Pumé families trickle over two or three households at a time, *everyone* raced around packing and loading goods and catching chickens and puppies.

Some moving-day highlights: Eulogio with a carrying pole laden with sacks and taiyós full of household goods, a tiny puppy perched precariously on his shoulder, another yelping in a basket, and two more dangling from one hand; María Diachi marching steadfastly along with a big load of household goods on her head and a burning log in each hand, keeping the lit ends carefully away from her dress; Marcos Pala with one of our backpacks on his back and a brimming plate of fresh-cooked rice and noodles balanced in one hand; and Amelia loaded down with several huge taiyó baskets, a potful of rice, and two despondent hens being carried upside down by their feet.

Water is precious to us, as it's now far away from our wet season camp, and everyone brought as much as they could carry. Of course they timed the move beautifully; the last of us staggered into camp just in time for a torrential storm.

Right now Rusty, in a burst of domestic enthusiasm, is weeding in our yard and around the baby mango trees growing in our old trash pile. Trino's and Eulogio's families are hurriedly patching their dilapidated house roofs against the ferocious black clouds scowling at us from the northeast. P.J. and his two wives Amelia and María Luisa are building a spacious, sturdy new *nyurihó* right in front of our door, for the convenience of inquisitive menstruating women. Dionisia, who is on her period, sits stubbornly in the caved-in remains of the old nyurihó; she'd rather get soaked in the coming storm than break with tradition and move back into her own house.

Meanwhile, P.J. is hurriedly thatching the new hut with the unremitting help of little Chita, Docha María, and Domana, whose main tasks seem to consist of hopping onto and falling backward into the fresh thatch lying on the ground, and standing right behind P.J. so he can trip over them whenever he takes a step backward.

4/26/93   Late yesterday afternoon a bunch of women, boys, and old Corona shocked us by gearing up for a big mango trip; they normally go after mangos in the early morning because it's such a long hike. I threw my pack over my shoulder, whipped out my notebook, and ran after them, struggling to write at the same time. It was suffocatingly hot and humid, and all of us were pouring with sweat a few steps out of camp. Naturally, I was the only one who'd brought any water, and by the time we stopped for a rest midway my canteen had been drunk dry (by everyone but me). While the women caught their breath in the shade of a small stand of trees, the boys cut long mango-hooking poles from the branches.

After a few minutes we set off again, and when the mango trees came into view the hot, tired Pumé actually broke into a run! I jogged after them and we broke into three teams of about five people each, picking the hard green mangos in a frenzy. We whispered to each other where the good fruit were so the others wouldn't hear. I've never seen the Pumé so competitive, although it was more like sport than a fight. After we'd slid down the Meta riverbank to gulp a few handfuls of water, we clambered back up, tied down our loads, and set back across the grassy hills leading home. The setting sun cast our walking shadows long and thin in front of us.

The moon was a little pale smile in the night sky, casting dim, diffuse light, and after a while I stopped straining to see the trail and instead focused my eyes on the basket of the woman marching in front of me. Strangely, I didn't stumble much; in the dark, feet are smarter than eyes. Poor Corona, carrying a pole with about 120 pounds of mangos tied on, stepped into an armadillo hole and went sprawling.

The women, intent on getting home, only giggled and passed him by as he groped for spilled fruit in the dark. An hour later we stopped for a much-needed rest on a hilltop. Everyone was wiped out—it had been a busy day before we even started, and most of us were carrying loads ranging from 60 to over 100 pounds.

All of us breathed in the cool night breeze and sat without

speaking. Corona stood up against the stars, looking remote and powerful wearing only his loincloth. His old man's muscles, still prominent, made a rugged landscape of his arms, legs, chest, and buttocks. Diacricia sat nearby, her rumpled hair and wrinkled face absorbing the starlight, her taiyó basket gleaming faintly, her body almost invisible in the waving grasses.

Several soft sighs later everyone heaved to their feet and helped each other get their sacks and taiyó loaded. We trotted home to be greeted by P.J. and a few kids on the dark trail into camp. The kids swarmed excitedly around their tired mothers, snagging a few bitter green mangos to munch on. Rusty was waiting outside our house with a smile and a big cup of water.

4/29/93   Baby Ana now has a big recognition smile for me when-ever she gets brought over. It's nice to be able to beam at each

other for a while before we get down to the usual round of playing, bottle-feeding, and letting Rusty tickle her with his beard,
which is one of her favorite games.

Everybody's getting ready for tohé tonight. Now that the wet
season has started we can expect lots more dances; nearly every
other night someone pokes a smiling face in our house and says to
us, "Tohé ngwá!" "Dance tonight!" I don't know if it's because
there is less visiting activity and there are more folks at home to
participate, or if it's just because everyone is hungry, sick, or bored
during this time of year and restless for the fun and drama of the
ceremony.

As the shadows lengthen, I watch while everyone goes in shifts
to bathe and dress in their nicest clothes, and admire the girls as
they fix their hair in delicate braids at the forehead and the nape
of the neck. They paint each other's faces with red paint using
the plant onoto (or lipstick, if they can get it), and if there's enough
paint the little girls and babies are also made up.

The pattern can vary from simple spots on each cheek to a
complicated series of bars, vertical and horizontal, on the nose
and forehead. Rarely we've seen a beautiful, intricate spiderweb
pattern, but we don't know who the artist is. This is the only form
of two-dimensional art we've seen the women create. The men
carve toh kaereah tóh, or face-printing sticks, whose carved sur-
faces are smeared with paint and pressed onto the cheeks and
forehead.

At sunset everyone hangs their burí in the tohé plaza and chairs
and stumps are dragged out. People sit and catch up on the latest
gossip, the men smoking cigars and snorting nanú and the women
smoking and nursing babies. The kids race around laughing, singing,
screaming, wrestling, and staging play-dances. Even the married
teenagers sometimes indulge in pre-tohé kid madness.

Although the Pumé have no watches, the ceremony almost always begins between 7:30 and 7:45 P.M. The sponsoring couple go

to the front of the crowd, always facing east across the plaza, and sit, softly singing, the man creating each new verse and melody, and the woman echoing the chorus.

One by one men and women join in the couple's song, the men dragging chairs and stumps to the edge of the dance area and women sitting together on the ground, always to the right or south of the men. Everyone faces east. At about 11:00 P.M. or so, depending on the liveliness of the singer, the dancing starts. The men get up and run around the central pole in a scattered stampede. The women, hands around each others' waists, run around the pole, making a sweeping radius and always keeping the line straight, their feet trotting in perfect unison. Everyone continues to sing. I've heard the women do another, more complicated dance with lively hopping and a movement of the dance line something like crack-the-whip, but I've never seen it.

The sponsoring man decides when to take a break and the men line up again. The women join, standing to the right. The men echo the chorus of the sponsoring man, who stands bent over at the waist and shaking the rattle, which he's been doing continuously since he began to sing and will do until the sun rises. The women hold each other round the waist and do their swaying, hip-swinging, dance, feet fixed, and sing the chorus. After a while, the sponsoring man stops his song and the men all say, "Ó-ha", signifying the end of that round of singing. Some sponsors almost never dance; others, like Eulogio, dance so hard that Rusty gets blisters from running around the pole for hours.

Late in the night is the usual time for spirit possessions and the curing ceremony. As in curing ceremonies all over the world, the healer uses the sucking cure. He also chants and blows cigarette smoke, water, or blood on the patient. P.J. is the best healer in camp, but I've never seen him pull a cayman bone out of a patient in the way that more flamboyant Pumé curers do. I've heard that the criollos occasionally have themselves cured by their Pumé neighbors, if Catholic prayer and store-bought medicines aren't doing the job.

Just before dawn, the sponsor leads everyone to the east edge of the plaza where they sing the first light into the sky. It is a fast, rousing wakeup song, the way the dawn would sound if it had a voice. I can always identify it in my half-asleep state and realize that tohé is over. Afterward, people sit in the plaza and chat in the ringing silence, sometimes drinking manioc punch. The women then filter away with the children to start the morning fires and another day.

4/30/93 It's gotten to the point where the women, as soon as they find out that I'm menstruating, will keep an eagle eye on me to make sure I don't eat fish or other forbidden foods for the duration. On days when there's nothing but fish, Rusty will pretend to eat everything we're given, then secretly pick the bones out of half of it. He hides the fish and I casually walk over later and stuff the cold, congealed meat quickly into my mouth, swallowing without chewing.

Evening: The sun has coyly come out just before setting. High gray ice mists like pigeon down and rounded, dark-blue clouds like bubbles of enameled metal float together in a brittle, sweet yellow lemon-drop sky. The new grasses are a rich, brilliant green, and new flowers in bright childlike lavender and deeper, voluptuous violet have sprung up along the trails leading to the bathing pond. We had our first ripe mango of the season today, roasted with the crisp blackened peel sliding off of sweet, brown caramelized flesh.

5/1/93 Yesterday most of the women and a few men marched out of camp before dawn and returned at dusk laden with sacks and taiyó brimming with beautiful ripe mangos, red and gold and sweet-smelling. For about an hour after that the only sounds in camp were munching, slurping, and smacking punctuated by quiet conversation. Today, happy kids are wandering around with mangos in both hands, liberally smeared with sticky flesh and juice from head to foot. Under a steady flow of hints from the women, several boys and men went fishing today and got home with respectable takes, so everyone's mango-hands have turned into fish-hands and the starving dogs and puppies are competing fiercely for the scraps.

Although dogs are useful camp sentries and important helpers to the men while on the hunt, very few dogs ever survive to adulthood out here. Of the fifteen pups born last year, none survived. Out of sixteen pups currently in camp, only one or two look like they'll make it through the next few weeks. The reason for this is that there are simply not enough meat scraps. People eat so efficiently that the few bones left over are only enough for one or two adult dogs. In a place where kids rarely get enough to eat, people are not apt to feed dogs. I wish the Pumé would just kill pups they don't want, instead of letting them die slowly of starvation and disease.

My shoulders ache from hauling water from the wells about one-third mile south of camp. Storms are threatening, but little rain actually falls and the wells near to camp are still dry. Never again will I, as an archaeologist, blithely fill out a site form with, "nearest water, 1/2 kilometer away." Now that I have to haul water, I join the Pumé women in complaining about the distance. It's hard, unending work!

All the women are currently hauling ten or so gallons of water two-thirds of a mile at least twice a day. So next time I see an archaeological site where the nearest water source is over a quarter-mile distant, I'll guess that: (a) it was either a temporary camp, or (b) the water was nearer to the site in the past, or (c) the women were expecting a rise in the water table in the near future!

5/3/93 Now that the mangos are in season, a nice treat on a rainy day is mango pudding. I like this recipe because it uses up unripe green mangos, which are bitter, fibrous, and wear away your tooth enamel when eaten raw:

> Take five large or seven small mangos and boil them about 1/2 hour or until the skin splits open. Take the mangos off the fire and let them cool about 20 minutes. Remove the skins and scrape the flesh off of them using a dull knife or metal spoon. Discard the skins. Scrape the flesh off of the pits and discard the pits. Sneakily add 2–4 tablespoons of sugar to the cooked flesh (the greener the mangos, the more sugar you need) and stir thoroughly. Eat while warm. Serves 4.

As I was taking data in Dori's house the other day, I fell into musing about the popular misconception of American Indians as untamed, savage people. Even our neighbors the criollos think of the Pumé as wild and free (kind of like a race of children who never grew up), or as fierce (like wild animals). But when I watch my Pumé sister Dori sitting like a cat in her small, tidy home, utterly at peace sewing or cooking, I think of all things wifely and domestic. A North American housewife, clad in day-glo spandex and wielding a vacuum cleaner, would probably send Dori running in terror.

María Romero, the shy mother of the baby boy who died last month, chatted with me a little this morning. She looks healthier; her cheeks have filled back out and she's more cheerful. I'd guess she's recovering from José Ahi's death. But he was an autumn baby for her, as she's getting beyond the safe childbearing age. Until her goofy daughter Micheda gets married, there won't be any more babies in that household.

Just about all there is to eat these days is mango. During this transition time between wet and dry seasons, neither of the seasonal foods is available. The fish are dispersing, as the ponds expand and flow into each other, but the wild roots and garden crops haven't had enough rain to grow to harvestable size. Mango-picking, our only option, is no picnic; a bunch of people left at 4:55 this morning to harvest by the river. They were gone eleven hours and probably walked about seventeen miles round trip. They came in utterly exhausted and no wonder; Rusty and I weighed their take and calculate that about eighteen people brought in more than a half-ton of mangos.

Some of the babies were brought along so they could nurse during their mothers' long day out, and it was fun to watch José Rahe and Dionisia María return, perched triumphantly on top of their mothers' brimming taiyós of fruit. Many of the ripe mangos burst on the long trip and the wrinkled, dusty, sweaty grandmas were hobbling around camp trailing the fruit's sweet scent after them. Little Ana had been left behind, as she's too young to travel, and her grandmother Lucrecia watched her all day and fed her a little rice gruel. As soon as María Florenzia got home, Ana was brought over, and I could hear happy sucking sounds as she got her first breast milk of the day. Pumé babies get used to hunger early.

5/5/93   I've noticed all of Diacricia's daughters and granddaughters have inherited her wide face with large eyes, soft cheeks, and a tiny chin. Dionisia María, Dinah, and Chita all have lovely sweet faces, which look angelic even when covered with dirt and fish or distorted with angry crying. And sometimes when old Diacricia's smoke-cured, wrinkled face blossoms into a smile, you can see a beautiful young Pumé girl behind her eyes.

5/7/93   Most of the men have gone away to a more distant ranch, this time for three weeks, and their families are tightening their belts. The criollo ranchers are hiring the Doro Aná men more and more often, because the Pumé value goods more than wages and will accept the food and tobacco given to them during wage work as part of the pay.

An adult man will typically return home with three days' worth of food and some used clothes for several weeks' hard labor. Meanwhile, their wives have supported the families on whatever they can gather in between child-tending, water hauling, sewing, weaving, cooking, and firewood chopping. While the men are better-fed during their work period, the women and children are worse-fed, and the deficit is never made up. The sexual division of labor, whose two aspects normally contribute jointly to Pumé subsistence, causes a direct conflict of interest to arise between women and men whenever Pumé men receive offers of wage labor.

Wage work is an increasing trend, and I can see how it forces the Pumé away from the mobile foraging lifestyle; as the men go away more often, their hungry families will eventually have to move to the river area, where the women can cadge a little food or work in criollo houses and fields. In this way, the Venezuelan government, by merely encouraging more criollos to settle here, slowly squeezes the Pumé off their ancestral lands, and incidentally increases the criollo need for dirt-cheap Pumé labor.

I feel so powerless to help. Rusty says we are doing our tiny bit by giving tools, medicine, and small goods to the Pumé, and giving reports to the Venezuelan government describing the Pumé's situation and our recommendations for the future. The government, however, is under no obligation to act on these reports, or even read them.

We could devote ourselves to the back- and heartbreaking job of fighting the government, the oil, agriculture, and beef corporations, and the Park Service in a desperate effort to protect the Pumé's right to their way of life. But this would cut us off at the knees; the Venezuelan government would never grant us permits to study here again. If I think too much about this I feel frenzied, like tearing my hair out. At times I need to pull myself forcibly away and watch the small things going on around me, children playing or women grooming, to regain my sanity.

This morning P.J, María Llovina, and Amelia came over for a

chat and spotted a taranyuná, or deer-hunting hat, that Dionso had traded to us. To make these hats, men carve a piece of wood to resemble a stork's head and beak, which is singed in the fire to blacken it. The women weave a small cap and tie the wooden head into the top, then sew black cloth around the cap. The result is a black hat that looks tolerably like a stork's head from a distance. To hunt deer, men wear white shirts and tie on these hats, then stalk through the grass using the stork's jerky, stooped gait. Believe it or not, deer are often fooled by this, allowing men to get within shooting range.

P.J. took the hat down for inspection, then tried it on. The wooden headpiece, which was much too heavy, fell slowly forward into his face. This brought on a fit of giggles that infected all of us, partly because the wilted taranyuná looked so obscenely funny, and partly because it was such a good example of Dionso's lousy craftmanship. P.J. sat down and rewhittled and resinged the whole thing, and now it balances a bit better.

5/8/93   Fresh baby moriche leaves smell almost exactly like spring lilacs, and when you work with them the delicious fragrance stays on your hands.

A *chinakarú* gathering trip: I set out after Rufina and Diacricia early in the morning and a bunch of bored little girls trotted along after us. A herd of cattle surprised us on the path and moved really close, which made the Pumé nervous. I was walking behind Rufina and let out a whoop to scare the cattle away. The cattle paid no attention but Rufina leaped about three feet straight into the air, and everyone had a good laugh over it.

We came to the doró, which has risen dramatically in the last few days, and met Encarnación and Corona lancing the water with arrows to catch yegupái fish. The fish, having languished in tiny isolated pools all summer, are now swimming furiously through the connecting shallows in search of food and mates for the wet season spawn, which affects all llanos fish species simultaneously. We left the girls there and walked on through the pearly gray morning, the old women catching up on the latest gossip.

When we spotted a couple of promising chinakarú trees, Diacricia hacked away at the branches with a machete so we could reach the crescent-shaped, silver-furred wrinkly brown pods. We harvested for several minutes, pausing to chop more branches and finally to fall one of the trees. We then wandered through the woods along the creek, collecting bobuí leaves for weaving and more chinakarú pods, amid soft, liquid birdsong reflected by the clouds hanging low over the creek.

As usual, I spotted for Rufina, whose cataracts have almost completely blinded her. I like being entrusted with the duty of acting as Rufina's "eyes"—I also helped both women harvest bobuí leaves that were too high for them to reach. It's relaxing going gathering with the old women now. They're so used to me they hardly bat an eyelash when I scramble after them as they march out of camp. I sometimes forget that I am recording some of the last wild plant-gathering to take place on earth.

Chinakarú grow up and down the creek bed, in trees that are often just high enough so the pods are out of reach, but not big enough to climb safely. It's a common practice to hack off branches to get at the pods, which enclose pale, crescent-shaped seeds that look like almonds. The outer shells are horrendously bitter, and there is really no other way to shell them except with your teeth. So Rusty and I hawked and spat our way through my small batch of them yesterday, and were rewarded for our green teeth by a half-potful of savory chinakarú stew.

The seeds are boiled for about an hour to make a delicious thick broth, with the seeds themselves softening up like beans. They are fast becoming my favorite llanos wild food. We almost never get chinakarú on shareout, and now I know why; after the ordeal of shelling them, we want the stew all to ourselves!

Today Rusty and I went out after more, and spent a very pleasant day picking, shelling, cooking, and eating a big potful. The Pumé ran over when we got home with two small sacks full of pods and nudged each other, saying "*No indanéh!*" "An infinity of them!" They asked us where we'd got them and I pointed west, saying nonchalantly, the good trees aren't far. I think they were impressed with *us* for a change.

5/11/93   Our criolla neighbor Lu, whom I'd heard has returned home to her no-good husband Daniel, came over yesterday afternoon with a big batch of beef and rice and told us her family is headed upriver for the rainy season. It was the first time I'd seen her since her desperate flight to La Victoria, and she looks healthy and cheerful. More tellingly, she has recovered her air of sly good humor, which had vanished in her humiliation over the beating. I guess she has worked something out with her husband after all. She certainly has no options aside from him right now.

We kissed goodbye and she walked off with her baby boy, carrying some band-aids, antibiotics, and vitamins that we put in a bundle for her at short notice. I hope we meet again sometime; I really feel that she's a new friend.

Rusty's and my big chinakarú feast two days ago made such an impression on the Pumé that the following morning several young women and girls ran off to the same area to get some for themselves. It's the only time that we have been "trendsetters" for the Pumé on their own turf. Unfortunately, the women came back with very little of anything. Maybe chinakarú-picking requires the longer attention spans of old women or hungry niwéi.

The wet season plants are about a month ahead of where they were last year. The trips I've made to the doró have been just like they were last June, with mature tochó pods on the trees and the occasional sweet, soft yellow *gabaechó* fruit rotting under the bushes in the grass or bobbing in the water. Tochó are too bitter for me to enjoy, but ripe gabaechó taste like butterscotch and I scramble to grab them when I spot them, just like the little kids.

Hooray! At last the water table has risen and we have two new platform wells right next to camp; no more long hikes. The women celebrated yesterday by doing huge batches of laundry, including hammocks and mosquito nets. They are continuing today, and the cheerful sounds of slapping and swishing mingle with the snores of the men sleeping after tohé last night.

During tohé, which was held in P.J.'s house due to rain, we heard a heavy, muffled Splat!, "Oof!" and a chorus of laughter. Sometimes the Pumé don't tie their burís up securely and a load of kids will hit the ground like a ton of bricks.

5/18/93   The odds and ends of cloth the Pumé use to make their clothing sometimes come clear from the Caribbean coast, and include lots of U.S.-made junk. Little Teresa is wandering around in a T-shirt emblazoned in English with "No Pay Makes A Housewife." How uniquely appropriate here!

One of our favorite games to while away the hours when I have a cold and am staying in the hii (which is often these days), is mantis-baiting. Rusty will catch a small praying mantis (with the tongue-twisting name of *uihurúhuda*) and put her on the hii netting. I put a fingertip on the netting from the inside, which attracts several mosquitoes. I then trail my fingertip along the netting toward the waiting mantis, and the mosquitoes jostle each other, following me. They are so intent on the smell of blood, they don't even see the mantis and often actually stumble onto her.

She flashes out her arms like jade lightning and catches a mosquito, eating it slowly for several minutes. Then we start again. I sometimes get bitten on the fingers, but it's worth it; some days we have caught up to eighteen mosquitoes this way. It's amazing the lengths we'll go to for a little entertainment . . .

As I struggle to learn how to weave, the Pumé women keep

track of my slow progress. Today a big group of women and girls were visiting in our house and little Manisanta pointed out a new paintó fan I'd woven, stuck in the roof to dry. Everyone passed it around, and blind Rufina fingered it. "*Handí areáh!*" "That's how to weave!" she announced loudly. Words cannot convey my infinite smugness.

Late this afternoon I heard Eulogio shout, "Don't! Don't!" and saw Dionso, his troublesome nephew, marching out behind one of the houses with a machete. Seconds later we heard loud screams from José, Dionso's little son, who came stumbling out into the plaza—Dionso had beaten him with the flat of the machete for some misdeed. José ran over to the menstruation hut to cry by his mother, and his father hightailed it out of camp. The women gathered around to lift poor José's shirt and look at his bruises. María Florenzia came to our house holding Baby Ana and solemnly assured us that Dionso had done something *very* bad.

It's the first violence we've seen here. Pumé children are usually shamed into good behavior, and are only rarely pierced with the stingray spine when nothing else will work. Beating is impulsive, criollo-style discipline, and the Pumé frown on it. Needless to say, women are never beaten here. Dionso took a shovel and some string along with him on his way out, as if he were going to work in his garden, but we all know he's just avoiding the rebukes he's got coming to him.

5/25/93   At long last the men who were working for the distant ranchers have returned. Some visitors have also arrived, including the oldest Pumé in the area. "Old Grey," whom we've secretly named for his bushy silver hair, is about 80 years old, impressive in a people whose life expectancy (excluding infant mortality) appears to be 55–60 years. His arms and legs are very wrinkled, but his eyes and ears seem to be in good shape. Although he's certainly beyond the age for energetic hunting, he always hikes the four miles over from his home village armed with bow and arrows.

Sometimes he's accompanied by a very old woman, probably his wife, who's even more wrinkled than he is and covered with white splotches from "*pinto,*" a local skin disease. I'd like to talk with her, but she doesn't know me and plays hard-to-get. Old Grey, though, always treats Rusty like another of his numerous grandsons; before he heads home he always walks stiffly across the plaza, peers in under the our thatch, blinks a few times, works his old mouth, and informs us "*Ba kodí*!" "I'm leaving!" in a hoarse voice.

5/26/93   One of my favorite Pumé stories is one of Trino's. One morning after tohé he related a stork-hunting story that was very different from the "mighty hunter" tales the younger men are fond of telling.

> So I sneaked up, and I shot! and the arrow went under the wing, like this! [He mimes it going under his arm.] And the next one went right over his head like this! [Whoosh! goes his hand.] And the next one went past his butt, like this! [Another gesture.]

Finally, he said, he got so exasperated that he just stood up and threw his bow at the stork, which flew leisurely off.

Yesterday, as I was hiking to the ranch alone, I saw out of the corner of my eye a large snake's head lying in the grass at the side of the trail. Mindful of coral snakes, rattlers, and pit vipers, I leaped away. When I tiptoed back to get a better look, I was delighted to see a gorgeous baby boa constrictor. About five feet long and thick as my forearm, its bright rust-red body was decorated with pale yellow blotches rimmed with black. It had just shed its skin and was glossy and brilliant, a living jewel in the soft grass. Since the Pumé loathe all snakes and would undoubtedly kill it if they came across it, I tickled its tail until it slithered slowly out of sight.

As the waters rise relentlessly with the rains, the animals are on the move to higher ground, and we've been seeing signs of our new neighbors. Yesterday Rusty and Dos Pasos came across large, fresh jaguar tracks down by the creek, and last night the chickens raised the alarm. Cautiously, P.J. went out and shot a big, weird marsupial in the trees outside his house. It's a carnivorous relative of the opossum, larger and heavier in the body, with a long half-naked tail, short ferocious face, and grizzled brown fur. It's called *toh yowa réh* and the Pumé don't like it; they buried it far from camp.

Yesterday we got a good scare when Francisco's family brought Rufina in from the other camp on a stretcher made of a burí strung on a carrying pole. She was weak and faint, and like most old Pumé in pain, she had tied ropes tightly around her arms in a series of loops (we still don't know how that helps). She was brought into P.J.'s house, laid carefully on the floor, and covered with cloths to keep her warm. P.J. sat on the floor behind her and she settled into him like a human chair, taking comfort from his warm young man's body and from his healing chants and frequent blowings into her ear. They talked off and on for hours, he asking questions and she answering in a querulous chant interrupted by hysterical shallow breathing.

All we could do was sit nearby with the Pumé crowded around, all of us looking worried. Rufina is the oldest woman in camp, probably in her mid-60's, and although we couldn't find any clear symptoms we wondered if she might be in serious trouble. But she sang the *anyikui tohé*, the woman's song, all night in a tiny voice, and today she can walk with help. It looks like she's weathered another storm.

I now realize that the focused attention of everyone in camp, and of P.J., in particular, was an important part of the cure. I hope when I am a sickly old woman that I'm not dumped into a lonely, sanitary hospital bed. I'm sure I'd recover quickly surrounded by my rowdy family and a handsome young fellow to hold onto me, sing to me, and blow in my ear.

A New Friend
in the Llanos

5/30/93 It's time to pick up Chuck Hilton, a friend and colleague in physical anthropology from the University of New Mexico, who will be studying the Pumé and living with us for the next three months. We caught the last truck trip of the dry season, riding into town with old Don Armando and his son Chi-chi on a cattle drive.

Because we had to keep the slow pace of the cattle, it was a grueling three-day trip with little food, many downpours, and a few hours' sleep snatched in soaking wet clothes. The cowboys, or *ganaderos,* were bone-tired by this morning; they've had to herd cattle in fierce storms and over flooded creeks for six days. And for a week's backbreaking work each man will be paid the equivalent of $7.50 total.

Still, it was breathtaking to see a real cattle drive on horseback—no one has done it in the United States for decades. The cowboys looked so peaceful each morning in the glowing orange sunrise as we followed them out into the dew-sparkling grass. Each man slouched easily on his tough little criollo horse, with woolen poncho, weatherbeaten shapeless hat, plastic rain *gaucho* rolled and tied onto the saddle, and black tasseled knife sheath dangling against his thigh. Most of the cowboys rode with woven sandals, called *alpargatas* and spurs, or plain bare feet with spurs. The men, horses, and sleepy cattle were always washed in a gentle light diffused by the morning mist as they headed slowly out onto the broad, grassy back of the llanos.

This morning they drove the herd across another flooded *caño,* or creek. Crossings are electrifying, with the men yelping and growling at the cattle and muscling them into a run using their horses' weight and brute force. With the momentum built up by a dead gallop the cattle thunder into the swirling brown water, holding snouts high and snorting as they swim. Rusty and I usually perch on the truck or in a tree to avoid being trampled. Men in canoes make sure the cattle don't stray in the water, and two cow-

boys waiting on the opposite bank keep track of the animals as they heave blowing and shaking onto the sand.

Every night we slept and ate with the cowboys while Don Armando and Chi-chi were treated more formally. Although it's been rough, I prefer it that way. After a supper of a mango or two and a cigarette, we'd hang our hammocks and settle in for the night, the sleepy, mellow voices of the men growing silent with the vanishing dusk. Today we all arrived in town hungry and tired, with colds from being in wet clothes for days on end.

6/28/93   Early Sunday morning Rusty and I, unable to reach anyone by phone and not really sure whether Chuck had actually made it, walked to the little San Fernando airport in a strong breeze and glittering morning sunshine. We waited tensely inside until the plane landed, and I jumped up and ran to the window; whether Chuck had been able to come meant not only the success of his own project but was key to our own ability to continue working in Venezuela. My illness and our stay in town had been paid for entirely by loans from my parents. We had been out of money and supplies since January, and Chuck was to bring a much-needed infusion of both.

When we spotted him walking down the stairs out of the plane, it was a real adrenaline rush—we all hugged and shouted and laughed, making a scene in the small crowd of drowsy passengers. During the frenzy of buying goods for the Pumé, we've been getting used to each other, hearing all the news and gossip from home, carefully going over accounting, and introducing Chuck to criollo cuisine. It is strange to speak English with someone other than Rusty. It's even stranger to watch Chuck absorbing all the details of this place, and to help answer his questions; suddenly I've leaped forward from the position of the novice to that of an old hand.

Street scenes in a little Venezuelan cowtown: I compare the merits of earrings in a display window with a young working girl, both of us with hungry eyes and empty pockets; I exchange pleasantries with a flirtatious young orange juice vendor and his cronies on a hot, slow afternoon; Rusty and I have a long chat with an Arabian hammock vendor, whose big-eyed wife carefully writes her name, "Sukkarieh", on the back of her business card and gravely urges, "Name your first daughter after me!"

6/14/93   We set off early on the morning of the 11th, and sat down at the river crossing at La Lechuga to wait for the Aguilars to show up. After a few minutes an old woman, her long, salt-and-pepper hair girlishly braided, hobbled up and asked us who we were. When we told her she wandered over to her tiny house nearby and returned holding a tiny female cayman.

It was about a foot long, brightly colored in gold, black, white, and jade green, its scales as smooth, warm, and pliant as the skin on a chocolate pudding. It had a delicate pointed snout whose mouth was open in the heat, its tiny needlelike teeth visible. The old woman bent over it, stroking it gently, her wrinkled brown face peering into the reptile's jewellike golden eyes. She told us she was going to raise it; I never asked her where she was going to keep it when it grew to its adult length of ten feet.

We spent a pleasant night at our friend Doña Petra's, where we were served a delectable supper of tapir in gravy over rice. Tapir meat is delicate yet rich, and is now my all-time favorite game. The next morning I helped Doña Petra cook up a big breakfast of *arepas* (corn fritters), scrambled eggs, cheese, and *café con leche*. It has been a real pleasure to be admitted into the smoky, sacred atmosphere of the kitchens of my criolla friends. A year ago I had to wait outside and eat with the men.

A typical criolla kitchen is a tiny, almost lightless adobe room with smoke-stained walls and ceiling and a tiny window high up. Women cook on a big wooden table whose surface is coated with adobe to make a perfect "stovetop." Wood fires are built on the hard-baked mud surface to cook meals. Another table holds a confused jumble of well-battered pots, pans, plates, gourds, cups, and silverware. Still another table usually holds vegetables, fruits, and bags of rice, sugar, coffee, pasta, and cornmeal. Dried meat and garlic generally hang from the roof or walls, and the dishes are washed in two buckets on a table outside. Our hostess Doña Petra has a beautiful kitchen, gratifyingly old, dark, and smoky.

During our trip home on the river we saw for the first time two troupes of howler monkeys leaping through the trees, one female with an infant clinging to her belly silhouetted for an instant against the pearly gray sky. For some reason, the river was teeming with freshwater dolphins, and Chuck was lucky enough to see dozens of them on his first boat trip. Roseate spoonbills perched in the trees on the bank, looking like creamy pink peppermints against the somber dark green foliage. And to my delight there were hundreds of hoatzins flopping clumsily through the trees, always choosing branches too small to hold them and flapping their bright rust-red wings wildly to keep their balance.

After a hectic day at the Aguilar's ranch buying food and repacking our goods, we got into Doro Aná late in the afternoon yesterday. I helped Chuck set up in his own tiny house, which the Pumé had built for him while we were in town. The Pumé amused themselves by crowding around to talk earnestly to Chuck, who couldn't understand a word.

Afterward, while I was tidying up our own house, María Luisa came over holding little José Rahe, who she said had very bad diarrhea. Not only was the baby sick, he was emaciated, a little skeleton with sunken, blankly staring eyes. His mother Chitaranyí stood uneasily nearby. Alarmed, I pinched the skin on José's shrunken belly. It stayed up in a little cone, indicating extreme dehydration. Every few minutes his eyes would roll up in his head, and he would sag into a faint.

Weeks ago, the day we'd left to get Chuck from town, José Rahe had toddled over to our house and peered in at us, his tiny face lit up with his goofy baby's smile. Then he noticed a stranger was sitting with us, a criollo boy from Moleto's place. The baby let out a loud wail of fear and I picked him up and carried him to his aunt's house, his little legs clinging strongly to my hip. It had been deeply gratifying to have him show us so openly that we are Pumé, and part of his family. Now he was within hours of irretrievable coma and death.

I shakily dissolved some gentle antibiotic in a little water with some sugar and eased a teaspoonful between his slack lips. He revived just enough to vomit it right back up. His mother came in and took him from María Luisa, asking me to rub ointment on his belly, which I did. José was beyond noticing anything we did for him, and his weeping mother wandered out of the house with him. I ran out to give her a bowl of rehydration formula I'd mixed up. José clenched his teeth against it and it went down his chest.

At home I paced and remembered José Ahi, who had died two months earlier because we had been away . . . abruptly I marched over to P.J.'s house, where they'd taken José Rahe to be cured. P.J.

was sitting outside with Amelia and María Luisa, the baby lying across his lap. The three adults were all crying quietly, P.J. occasionally blowing in José's ear and talking to him. Chitaranyí was nowhere to be seen. I steeled myself and knelt by P.J., asking María Luisa to fetch the rehydration drink I'd given to José's mother. When she returned with it, I pinched the baby's nose, and when he opened his mouth to breathe, I gently forced the drink down his throat.

This woke him up and he fought me, sputtering and gasping. I kept on for nearly an hour, talking to him and making a joke out of pouring the stuff down his gullet every time he made a face and opened his mouth wide to cry. P.J. started to laugh with me, and Amelia and María Luisa wiped their noses and watched.

This morning José Rahe is nursing for the first time in three days, and crying with some of his old energy. His skin is getting tighter, and after I got him started on the rehydration fluid this morning he kept drinking on his own. Later today he walked a few steps with María Diachi's help. Much as I hate forcing medicine on people, I think we bought him another chance last night. It's not over yet, though; with only one very young, inexperienced parent he and his sister have a long hard childhood ahead of them.

6/15/93 Last night I went over to give José Rahe a little more formula. His mother was cheerful for a change, and although he was very tired, he summoned up enough strength to give me the ghost of his clownish grin. Both his mother and I laughed, and it was one of the most piercingly sweet things that has ever happened to me, to see that little smile swim back up from the shadows.

6/19/93 It was a hot humid morning that has turned into a beautiful pearly gray afternoon, cooled by gentle rains. José Rahe came by to say hello, and he looks normal and comical as ever. We smiled at each other, and I gave him a sweet protein pill in tiny bites after first softening it with my own saliva. When some bigger kids came over, I drew on their arms with a magic marker: a dragonfly on Manisanta, a pirhana on Olga, and a cayman on Luis María. Big boy that he is, he was still tickled pink about his "tattoo" and ran off to show the other boys.

Chuck is working hard at understanding the language every day, repeating everything said to him by the laughing Pumé. When I watch him, I still feel a jolt of disorientation, as though I'd just waked up from a year-long dream. But I enjoy having someone else from my home country to talk to, and I think having his friend here has perked Rusty up considerably.

6/21/93   Yesterday 13-year-old César marched proudly into camp with an anteater strung on his bow and a bunch of kids trailing excitedly behind. They laid the spaniel-sized anteater on the ground and I took pictures of her; she was beige with a pretty black cape across her shoulders and a black stripe down her long, elegant snout. Old Victor pulled her long purple tongue out—it kept coming for about two feet. Anteaters look like broken toys when they're dead, peering weakly up from the sand with little fading button eyes, short soft fur gleaming, long tail curled coyly in death. In half an hour she was a potful of meat.

Afterward, while little Manisanta was perched in Rusty's chair, he pretended not to see her and sat down on top of her. She squirmed frantically as he squashed her, making her laugh in a series of strangled "*Ayah*'s!" Earlier today, taking advantage of a rare sunny afternoon, I was bathing and washing clothes in an old well next to camp. A bunch of little girls, headed by Newe, trooped down to dig a new well. They took turns digging, scooping and chatting with me, taking breaks to bathe and play in nearby pools.

A year ago adults and children alike would sneak peeks at my strange, pale body from a safe distance whenever I was bathing or changing clothes in sight of camp; in the wet season, we have no choice. Now the kids come down and keep me company just like they would with any aunt or cousin. Aside from a snake scare that sent pretty Newe bounding out of a pool, it was a pleasant, uneventful bathe in the sparkling sun and waving grass, one of the quiet things that fill in the spaces between data and drama in Doro Aná.

I wonder what the children will think of us when they grow up, how they'll remember us. In the eyes of the kids who were unborn or infants when the anthropologists Ted and Gay Gragson visited here four years ago, Rusty, Chuck and I stand alone like rocks sticking up from the grass: the only non-Pumé who have ever lived in Doro Aná. And baby Ana, José Rahe, and Juana Trina's Domana, who but for our help would not be alive, are small but growing testaments to our short stay here. Will people tell them about us when they're old enough to understand?

6/25/93   Today I went collecting baby moriche leaves by myself. As I approached the doró in full flood, I could see it was swollen way past the banks, its pewter flanks moving smoothly through the grasses on either side. I waded in confidently but in the middle realized I was losing my footing. The powerful current surged past my chin, pulling like a greedy living thing at my clumsy booted feet. I reached the other side out of breath, wishing I didn't have to cross back over.

But I picked a bunch of bobuí leaves in an atmosphere pleasantly charged with danger, and when the time came to cross again I only lost my footing once. When I got home, Lucrecia scolded me for going, saying that large caymans and anacondas live in the creek this time of year. Whether or not they really are lurking there waiting to snap up unwary female niwéis, I won't cross the creek alone in full flood again.

6/28/93   As the sun rose this morning, Rusty glanced over at me excitedly. "Psst! Pat and Dori are going out!" he whispered. Because their doorway is hidden from view from ours I almost never get a chance to follow Dori. I grabbed my sidepack and ran after them along the trail, rosy from early sunlight.

After investigating a few old tracks and armadillo holes we stood at the crest of the tallest dune to the south of camp, watching a glowing, sunlit column of rain approach us from the north. The sweet wind on the skirts of the storm blew the gnats away and I could see Pat thinking hard, wondering which route to take. His wife Dori stood quietly in her waiting mode, squinting a little in the fine, silvery rain that beaded in her hair and eyebrows. Finally, Pat said, let's go over that way, and pointed to the treeline far to the south, dark gray-green in the drizzle.

We hiked arduously across a flooded swale and onto another dune, where it looked like a bomb had blown a small crater in the sand; a Pumé man had dug up an *igurú* (armadillo) burrow there a few days before. We were about to leave when Pat pointed out a tiny hole in the backdirt, and probed it with the point of his lance. He then used the machete to dig out three baby armadillos, whose mother (and probably another baby—they are always born in quadruplets) had been killed by the earlier hunter. The babies had been trying to dig their own way out.

Dori gave me one. They really are exquisite; perfect small replicas of the adults, their little carapaces are soft as an infant's fingernail. As I held her up, my igurú writhed a little, turning her spoon-shaped ears this way and that, her tiny eyes filled with vague alarm. I left my animal-loving vegetarian lifestyle behind me long ago like a shed snakeskin, I reminded myself; I am a different person here. So before I could get too fond of her I whacked her against the axe handle, and she curled up and died.

We packed the babies up and continued south, catching a large electric eel and a colorful baby tortoise. So far, our catch was only about a pound or so of meat, but we doggedly checked all animal sign including several deer beds in the grass. We arrived at the

gallery forest at the edge of the doró, where Pat had an old garden. While he gathered *tuípa* (the mild hallucinogenic plant the
Pumé chew as an analgesic, much like our aspirin), Dori gathered
some twiggy firewood and we sat down for a while. Pat returned
with an armload of tuípa and he and Dori began scraping, roasting, pounding, and peeling it in the weak sunshine.

Dori and I were chatting softly when Pat shushed us and said
urgently, "There are deer over there! Two of them!" We continued
to process the tuípa as the deer, a large buck and a juvenile doe,
wandered closer. Pat murmured with tense annoyance that he
didn't have his *taranyuná*, or deer-hunting hat, and white shirt
along with him. As the deer approached, Pat soundlessly stripped
off his shirt so his brown skin would blend with the surroundings,
and grabbed his bow and lance-tipped arrow, or *niyatéh*, whose
head is shaped like a leaf. He ran in a crouch to a small bunch of
trees down wind of the approaching deer, then sat and watched
while Dori and I huddled low in the grass, our small fire still smoking and covering our scent.

The atmosphere had changed from drowsy to electric, Dori
whispering excitedly to me with sparkling eyes; it reminded me of
those intoxicating hide-and-seek games we'd played as children,
which in turn probably started as play-hunts uncounted ages ago.
Pat straightened up and waved vaguely at us. Dori held up the
machete questioningly. Pat's less-than-precise answer was to wave
more energetically. Dori and I looked at each other and shrugged,
lying back down on our elbows in the warm grass.

Pat gave up signing to us and stalked the deer slowly as they approached the edge of the tangled, overgrown garden a dozen feet
from where Dori and I crouched. Pat abruptly straightened up and
the arrow string sang hoarsely as it sent the niyatéh flying through
the air. I heard an anguished bleat as both deer exploded away, the
buck headed north into the grassy swale, the doe into the old garden. Pat came running and told Dori to take the machete and cir-

cle around to the southeastern edge of the garden. She ran off nimbly through the mud and was instantly out of sight in the brush. Pat spat a mouthful of Pumé at me, made another vague gesture and ran off in the opposite direction with his bow and remaining lances.

I stood in knee-deep water with my mouth hanging open, a wounded deer in the garden and two overwrought, hungry Pumé out of sight on either side of me. Had Pat meant for me to stay put? To follow him? To wait by the fire? To accompany Dori? After an anguished thirty seconds I moved cautiously along the garden's south edge, which I guessed neither of the Pumé could see from their positions. Trying not to make noisy splashes with my heavy boots, I strained my ears. I heard a tiny splash to my left, in the thick brush of the overgrown garden. It could be anything, probably a bird, I thought. But I quit moving and waited. Another cautious splash. I held my breath and let it out slowly.

Suddenly a golden animal burst from the bushes two feet to my left, bounding across the flooded grasses in an attempt to get to the thick forest about 100 feet away. I whooped and yelled, "Hey!! The little deer is here! HERE!" and charged after it, running top speed through the knee-deep water underlain by thick lumpy mud. That mud also worked against the little doe; already weak from the lance wound in her lower back, she stumbled and fell just a few feet away from the safety of the underbrush and lay there, panting.

I approached her—she was young, about the size of a large German shepherd. Her beautiful fur was brown with glittering gold highlights fading to a rich cream color at her belly, throat, and inner legs. She looked straight through me with huge, swimming eyes. To her, I didn't exist.

Dori broke the spell, running up and daintily whacking the fawn on the head twice with the machete, blows that wouldn't have hurt a fly. Pat raced up and ended it with a point-blank shot to the heart. The deer gave a bleating cry once more and her frothy blood pumped slowly out as she lay down and died.

As Pat dragged the deer back to our dying fire, the three of us talking and laughing loudly, my hands still shook with excitement. While the two of them butchered the deer, Pat proudly described over and over (despite Dori and me having *been* there) how he'd stalked and fired his arrow. It truly was a remarkable shot, even for a Pumé; it had covered twice the usual distance.

"But why," he panted as he carefully tore the golden skin away from the muscles, "didn't you guys fan the fire when I signaled to you?" Dori and I looked blank. "I was *signaling* to you to fan up the fire to scare the deer toward me!" Pat explained with exasperation. Dori and I exchanged a secret glance and grinned.

After an impromptu feast of roast baby igurú, tortoise, eel, and sumptuous fresh deer heart, liver, and lungs, we loaded up and set out for home, Pat marching proudly in front with the fawn tied onto his bow. On the trail Pat asked Dori, "Where did the deer break out and run?" And Dori replied, "I didn't spot it, *she* did!" And all of us laughed that I could actually have been helpful in the hunt.

7/3/93   The sun had decided to make a rare appearance today, and the rain-washed llanos sparkles like an emerald. While Pat was describing the escaped buck's antlers to his brother P.J., I was reminded of a postcard Chuck had sent us earlier this year, the classic southwestern "jackalope" photo showing a stuffed jackrabbit with pronghorn horns glued onto its forehead.

Rusty brought it out one day while the Pumé were visiting, and with a straight face showed it to P.J., saying, "There are horned rabbits where we come from!" P.J. looked skeptical but couldn't deny the photo. As Rusty went on to describe in rich detail the animal's habits, its ferocity and the tastiness of its meat, I kept snorting with laughter. P.J., always quick to pick up on atmosphere, kept looking from me to Rusty, wondering just how hard his leg was being pulled.

Although the waters have risen to normal flood levels and millions of yipái are waving their otherworldly fronds in the savanna, the Pumé women are not yet gathering wild roots. While the mangos are still in season, the Pumé are doggedly making trips to get them every couple of days or so. I remember how desperately I craved the sweetness of a little fruit last wet season, but our diet has been nearly pure mango for over two months now. Whether they are ripe, roasted, boiled, or green, I'm sick of them. But yesterday I went to the garden with Docharanyí and Chitaranyí, and promising tender baby chokuí leaves nodded their striped heads in the shady secret spots at the foot of every tree.

7/4/93   Chuck has begun collecting detailed body measurements, called anthropometrics, of all the Pumé. These measurements will provide information on Pumé anatomy and physical condition, including the malnutrition we need to inform the Venezuelan government about. We have decided to start off with the men, to let everyone get adjusted to this latest example of niwéi craziness.

The Doro Aná men's reactions have strongly reflected their individual characters: Dos Pasos was vaguely confused but benevolent, Eulogio full of jokes, Francisco dignified but smiling, Corona anxious to get back to his gardening, and P.J. burningly curious as to how and why we did everything we did. The teenaged boys were pretty predictable, tense and self-conscious while being measured, full of juicy comments and rude belly-laughs while other boys went through the ordeal.

All the women gathered in the menstruation hut to watch; the tiny doorway was filled to the roof with laughing faces. Whenever anything particularly hilarious happened (someone lifting his arms too high, or standing on the weigh scale too long), the women and girls would hoot with laughter and nudge each other joyously. I thought to myself, live it up girls, you're next.

7/8/93   This morning before dawn Rusty woke me up slithering out of the hii. "Why are you in such a hurry to get up?" I asked sleepily. "Oh, you know, it's good to be up and ready," he mumbled, rooting around on the shelf. He found a bundled-up T-shirt and pushed it under the edge of the hii. A tied bandana was also shoved in. "Open 'em up!" he said, swatting at the hungry morning mosquitoes. I opened the first and recognized P.J.'s beautiful tohé rattle, carved in loving detail. "Is this for me?" I asked unbelievingly. "Happy Birthday!" he answered with a grin. Inside the second bundle were three rolls of hammock nylon, sky-blue, coral-pink, and buttercup yellow. "I'll have María Llovina weave me a burí!" I gloated. Rusty smiled with satisfaction and swatted.

7/9/93   My birthday *chiyokodé*, or rattle, carved by P.J. around the time we arrived last year, is a beautiful example of Pumé workmanship. It has the common pattern of Pumé dancing with arms interlinked with some dancers holding their rattles. Several jaguars and a capybara walk amid large flower or sunburst shapes, and a strange human-shaped spirit straddles the top of the gourd, waving winglike or flamelike hands.

This afternoon P.J. is recounting for us the story of how bugs came into being. It's a Pandora's box kind of story, in which the inquisitive capybara opens a magic gourd and the biting insects escape to molest the entire world.

In the telling P.J. is using one of my favorite kinds of emphasis in Pumé speech, which is leaving a gap between the syllables of a word. For example, the term for "far away" is *hatchí*. "Very far away" is *hat — chí*, "really far away" is *hat . . . chí*, and so on. For truly interstellar distances P.J. will sometimes leave us in suspense for up to four seconds between syllables.

The bugs are in full wet season glory, swarming so thickly sometimes that they coat my glasses and I can't see through them. Once more the simple act of dropping my pants to pee requires a few seconds of mental fortification and always results in dozens of gnat and mosquito bites that sting and itch for days afterward, sometimes becoming badly infected. When I bathe in the little hole outside camp, I quickly cover myself in soap and the bugs lighting on me get stuck in the lather, so that by the time I'm ready to rinse I'm coated like a poppyseed bagel with dead soapy bugs.

Today the sun is a hot silver disc, tempered by the departing mists of an early morning storm. Baby mango, *onikorí* fruit, and watermelon plants stretch their tender necks upward from a trash pile that Rusty painstakingly weeded a few days ago. It's nice to think we'll have trees here someday—maybe if we return in our old age we'll be able to harvest mango and the sweet, crumbly-fleshed *onikorí* fruit from our very own trees!

It would seem that little kids are rude and gross no matter where you go. Naughty Docha María sings to herself all day long in a cracked, off-key voice reminiscent of her grandfather Vic-

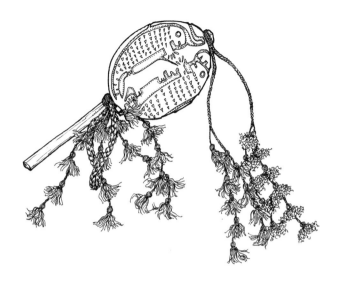

tor's; I can hear her right now: "*A-gurí a-guuurí, a-gurí a-guurí*" ("Go take a shit, go take a shit"), she warbles. This ditty is the least offensive of her repertory. As I learn more of the language, I find that those Pumé kid songs I used to think were so cute (and are indeed sung very tunefully) are either obscene, or scatological, or both.

7/12/93   In the eons that stretch before me on sleepless nights, tiny animal noises mark the passing time, about which my watch can tell me nothing. I stare up into the blackness and hatch a hundred brilliant schemes for learning how to weave, how to cook gourmet foods, methods for scamming money, masterpieces I will paint, write, sculpt.

I struggle to picture people's faces but they swim away in the dark like little fish. I wonder if my own face is similarly evading someone else out there—a friend or a family member trying to conjure me up in their memory on this long night.

7/13/93   Tohé plaza is so beautiful after an early morning rain: sand like a hammered silver sheet with the black burí poles writhing up toward a sky dark dusty purple, like the bloom on a grape. Bird-song is especially clear and liquid these moist, quiet mornings, as though the birds were perched on your burí with you, singing to you.

The day before yesterday little Chita fell into a fire and badly scorched the left half of her face, including the area immediately around her left eye. When they brought her to us, the eye was completely swollen shut and an enormous blister was weeping pus down her chin. I held her in my lap and talked to her while Rusty cleaned and dressed the ugly wound. After a lot of sobbing (the cleaning must have been very painful), Chita wandered away, still sniffling abjectly. Her rolling walk, due to her crooked leg, wrenched at my heart.

About an hour later I spotted her walking aimlessly near the edge of camp, all bandages gone, her little hand scratching miserably at the burnt side of her face. Her mother was nowhere in sight. Rusty was furious to see nearly half an hour's worth of pain-staking work ruined, as well as the blister itself clawed open. I caught Chita and pulled her into my lap again, and she began crying again immediately.

In spite of her struggles we dressed the wound again, but she moved with her mother to a neighboring camp for a couple of days and we couldn't keep track of her. So imagine our surprise when we sighted her this morning actually skipping in front of our house, her face healing beautifully! Treating Pumé kids for wounds and illnesses is always a mixture of bad and good surprises; they couldn't be less cooperative, but their healing powers are absolutely incredible.

7/15/93   Rusty, Chuck, and I took a day off and walked to the ranch to buy a few goodies. From the start, it was a great day for exotic bugs. A few minutes out of camp I spotted a gorgeous re-duviid, or "true bug," with a diamond-shaped body and long ele-gant head armed with powerful piercing and sucking mouthparts tucked under its chin, ready to flash out at the first sign of a victim. Its legs were black and its glossy, inch-long body was strikingly marked in geometric patterns of red, beige, and black with creamy golden highlights, making it look like a tiny, animated Hopi pot.

Its close cousin, the assassin bug, also lives in this area and is the carrier of the dreaded Chagas disease, a form of New World sleeping sickness that is incurable and fatal. The young naturalist Charles Darwin, in *The Voyage of the Beagle*, describes how the insects crawl onto sleeping humans and pierce the skin, especially around the neck, in order to suck the blood. The disease, transmitted through the saliva of the bug, takes years to kill its victims. Darwin died in late middle age, exhibiting terminal symptoms of Chagas disease.

On a little hummock in the middle of the flooded savanna Rusty pointed out a huge female spider crouched uneasily in the grass, waiting for us to pass by. She was about three inches in diameter and neatly furred like a mouse. Her head and thorax were fawn and white with black stripes, her dainty legs a deep chocolate brown. We couldn't see her abdomen because it was carpeted with tiny brown babies hitching a ride.

On our way home we stopped at a lovely forested hill, inside which was set, like a jewel in velvet, a pond teeming with turtles. Among the trees around the rim stood giant cacti, their spindly forms otherworldly in the slanting shadows of late afternoon. As Chuck and I sat peacefully in the shade munching crackers, Rusty came across a number of giant moth cocoons in a small thicket. We'd already seen a few of the pupae, a Pumé delicacy; each big brown body folds secretly in on itself, every detail of legs, face, and antennae etched in exquisite detail on the outer casing, like a tiny mummy. The Pumé eat them raw, and as with the palm beetle larvae, they are sweet and creamy inside.

Now we were delighted to see a large, newly emerged moth

hanging on a leaf next to a split chrysalis. The moth was entirely covered in tawny golden fur, dense and soft like a teddy bear's; its antennae were thin and bright yellow, and its huge feltlike wings each had a white Y-shape drawn on. Its fat abdomen glowed orange under the beige fur. As we watched, it hunched shyly on its leaf, staring fixedly at its furry front feet as though willing us to go away and leave it in peace. After admiring and photographing it, we left the moth to finish the slow process of pumping its tender, crumpled wings to full size with blood.

As we approached camp I spotted a flash of bright blue and almost passed it by, thinking it to be a piece of plastic. On closer inspection it turned out to be a large weevil beetle, its whole body and legs colored neon turquoise, punctuated by fat black spots. It looked cheerful and clumsy, like a clown. After I set it down and began walking away I could still see it glowing as if by its own light in the darkening evening.

7/16/93 Poisonous snakes have been finding shelter from the rain in our gardens and houses. This morning while I brewed tea we heard an uproar across camp, with Victor stomping and yelling and María Diachi whooping in a high, anxious voice. After a brief pause Victor marched proudly over to our house to show us the snake he'd killed. I was impressed with his skillful dispatch of the lightning-fast little pit viper—Victor has vision in only one eye.

As Vic approached our house, he held the snake out in front of him on the end of a stick. Little José, preceding him, kept looking nervously backward and of course tripped and sprawled right in front of the dangling corpse. Vic shoved it at the boy, who writhed away, terrified but giggling. As it lay on our floor, a tiny golden curl blending in with the color of the sand, Rusty pried open its jaws with a stick to expose two needlelike fangs. It's the second *Bothrops atrox*, or pit viper, we've seen in a house. I'm not too happy at the prospect of finding one of the pretty, deadly animals in *my* house or trash pile. Vic, determined to get all the mileage he can out of the incident, is now chasing José around camp with it, the two of them whooping, laughing, and shrieking.

7/17/93   Measuring the women for Chuck's anthropometry project has been going smoothly. Even Carmen Cartoria and Gusha, both hugely pregnant, have resignedly stood on the scale, sat on the stump, raised their arms, and hiked their skirts while I fumbled with the anthropometer. This instrument measures the dimensions of Pumé bodies, which will give us detailed information on their bone structure, fat content, overall health, and the ways in which their walking great distances makes their bodies develop differently from ours.

Pumé skin is very warm and very taut. When not bumpy with bugbites it is satiny smooth and mostly hairless. All the women, from toddlers to grandmas, have a special musk—it's a blend of smoke, sweat, baby pee, old go loincloths, hair oil, and fish. I find it a comforting smell. It reminds me of all the wounds I've treated, hearths I've sat near, kids I've tickled, babies I've held. It reminds me of helping María Florenzia give birth. It is the most human, growing, healthy smell I've ever smelled.

7/18/93   Although it's the middle of the wet season and fish are scarce, the men have decided it's a good day to go fishing—they've stormed us for hooks and line all morning. Their total catch: a couple of goldfish-sized *yegupái*. But I've noticed that the Pumé have a real herd instinct; one person will do something, and the next thing, the whole camp jumps onto the bandwagon, whether it's fishing or the first good harvest of wild roots. I recall all the oratory in North American politics about individuality and independence being the original human condition (from which the Old World and the Third World have supposedly degenerated). The Pumé show a subtle, complicated mix of free will and conformity: *you* decide what you're going to do, but you often end up copying the actions of people around you in hopes of a similar, or better, result.

7/21/93   Just as we'd sighed with relief that Chita's face has begun to heal, José managed to spill a potful of boiling water on Docharanyí's tiny baby girl. She's got second degree burns all over the right half of her body, from elbow to ankle. The pain must be incredible. María Diachi was furious and orated loudly in a high voice while we tried to bandage her grandaughter.

The baby's parents are just short of panicked by the accident—Docharanyí, whose face has always had a sad look in repose, is now genuinely subdued and worried, and Eulogio has been curing the baby by blowing on her and singing every few hours. The baby herself has hardly fussed at all. We heard her initial squawk of pain and surprise when the accident happened, and she frets when Rusty cleans and dresses the burns, but only out of restlessness. I am amazed by that little baby; not only is she healthy, pretty, and cheerful, but brave and tough too.

A creamy blue-black storm arches its back and sharpens its claws on Don Armando's pastures to the north. Little breezes tumble and pounce kittenishly through camp, cooling and sweetening the air. Lying in my hii I am grateful for the coolness of the storm-edge; the last three days have been breathlessly hot and still.

7/22/93   Last night I was awakened out of a deep sleep by a roaring, thunderous noise. The burí was shaking and I thought it must be Rusty shifting around. Then I heard the chickens squawking nervously in the trees—the house was wiggling strongly and regularly. It was a very dark night; the moon was a tiny fingernail clipping. The roaring and shaking woke the Pumé, who started to yell from house to house, "*Daburú haipá!*" which I took to mean, "It's an earthquake!"

After about two minutes, the tremors stopped. A strange breeze blew through camp, and the night returned to its usual hot calm. I was thoroughly scared and it took a long time to get back to sleep. Thinking back on it, I'm really glad we were in a sturdy, flexible house made of lightweight materials . . .

Docharanyí's baby girl is healing beautifully from her burns, her deceptively tender-looking baby skin knitting quickly and sloughing off the dried blisters. Miraculously, it looks as if she won't even have a scar!

7/23/93   After several days' debating, Rusty and I have decided I should go home a few weeks early. Although I'd healed pretty well from all the illnesses in the spring, I seem to have picked up hookworm in the last few weeks. My chest constantly aches, I have persistent diarrhea, and my symptoms of anemia are returning. I'm certainly not getting any work done.

I worry about which of the old Mothers and Fathers will be gone when I come back. Out of all the Pumé, I feel so much affectionate respect for the old ones, who spent their youths in loincloths before the advent of the outboard motor, the truck, the radio to the llanos. Part of me tries to soothe myself by saying, "The Pumé would tell you the new people are born and the old ones die to make room for them. Kumanyí's country up in the sky is so much nicer than down here, anyway."

The earth is called *Gito má*, or the realm of pain. After you die you go to Kumanyí's country, where there's enough food for everyone and pigs, horses, and cattle for all Pumé. So why be sad when an old, tired Pumé goes there? But when I lie here at night I can see their smoke-cured, sun-browned smiling faces, thinking they must soon leave us, and I want to cry like a little kid. How can they go away? Who will take care of us, who will feed, soothe, amuse, reprimand, and teach us when they've gone?

The Long Way Home

7/26/93   Of course I'd been imagining my final leave-taking of Doro Aná for months, and of course it was nothing like I thought it would be. We decided to wait until the last minute to tell the Pumé I was leaving, since they would otherwise wander in and out of the house for weeks asking "How many days (hours, minutes) until you go?" which drives us both crazy.

Yesterday morning P.J., Amelia, María Diachi, and María Florenzia were sitting in our house, chatting and keeping an eye on various babies rolling around on the sandy floor. During a pause in the conversation I told them I was going home. I explained that I had worms in my belly, I was tired all the time, and I was crying for my family in *Uí Aná Rupéh*, far away.

Far from being surprised, they nodded calmly. I actually got the impression they'd been waiting to hear it! They walked out of the house to spread the word around camp. Chuck and Rusty insisted on some farewell photos, so I ran around to each house and told the women, "I'm going home, so come quick and get photographed with me!" Lucrecia was the first to show up, resplendent in a patterned blue, white, and purple dress made from fabric Chuck had given her. She looked like a gnarled, weathered embodiment of a hearth goddess, beaming with her nearly toothless mouth when we ooh'd and ah'd over her fancy seamwork.

The other women took one look at her and vanished in all directions to change into *their* fancy new dresses, returning like a swarm of bright butterflies: María Florenzia in a matronly navy-blue, Amelia in brilliant marigold, Chitaranyí in a cheerful floral, and my favorite, María Diachi in neon pink that was so bright it brought a flush to her dark, wrinkled face and arms. I joked with them, "Hey, *I* don't have any nice clothes like you, just these dirty pants full of holes!" They giggled shyly while Chuck photographed them and the kids swarmed around our feet.

While we packed afterward, María Florenzia sat with baby Ana, both watching solemnly. "Remember to bring your daughter some clothes, and beads too, when you come back," María reminded me. "And formula!" She held the baby girl up and spoke softly into the tiny, velvety ear: "Your *aibuí* (little mother) is leaving, going far away, to *Uí Aná Rupéh*!" Ana blinked at me, her mouth open. Docharanyí came in and held *her* tiny baby up so she was looking straight at me. "This is your *aibuí*!" Docharanyí told her. "She's going far away and won't be back till you're able to walk!" The little baby, still in bandages, blew a few bubbles and suddenly gave me a radiant smile.

While the baby boys Batida and José Rahe climbed all over me, I told them I expected them to be catching lots of fish by the time I returned. They responded by getting into a dirt-throwing fight that degenerated into screaming and eye-jabbing. I disentangled myself and walked around camp, poking my head into doorways and saying my last goodbyes. Everyone said, "*Manabí*!" "Come back!" Then Chuck, Rusty, and I shouldered our packs and hiked off into the savanna, a few Pumé adults and the little girls standing at camp's edge under darkening rain clouds, watching us go.

I had known it was going to be hard to say goodbye. I'd pictured myself hugging the women while clutching baby Ana to my breast, heroically choking back the tears. But although I'd been on the razor's edge of crying during my last few hours there, I just couldn't. The Pumé save their tears for death, the last journey; if I'd cried in front of them, it would have distressed or amused them. Instead, I kept my affectionate maulings to the babies, and although my heart was squeezed by a strange, deep sadness unlike any I've ever felt before, I walked out of camp smiling. For them.

7/28/93 If the savanna was trying to leave me with one last fond memory, it failed. When it wasn't pouring rain so hard we couldn't see our own feet, the mosquitoes swarmed around us so thickly that each of us moved inside of his or her own column of bugs. But as we approached the ranch the curdled purple of the receding storm clouds set off the silvers and pale greens of the drenched llanos below, and an ice-white egret stood on a hill like a ghost, watching us wipe the rain off our glasses.

I've been at Hato San Jacinto by myself now for several days, waiting until we can leave for town by boat. I sleep in the beautiful burí María Llovina wove for me; it's bright yellow, blue, and pink, and smells like smoke from María's hearth. I like to lie here cradled by Pumé craftmanship, even if the Pumé aren't nearby.

7/29/93 This morning a ground mist was lying on the east pasture. When the sun rose, it filtered through the mist and washed the grass and the air just above in the oldest, deepest gold stained with rose. All it lacked was a coating of fine cracks to make it look as if the llanos had been painted by some old Italian master.

I've stayed at this ranch off and on, in sickness and in health, for over a year and I've formed changing opinions of its people. The ranchers are true criollos, or mixed-breeds, a hardworking, durable blend of Spanish, Indian, and Caribbean African ancestry.

Don Armando, around 70 years old, is the owner of the ranch and the founder of the Aguilar dynasty. He has skin burnt dark brown and leathery, nicely set off by his bright silver hair and mustache. He sees the world through thick glasses that magnify his tiny black eyes. There is a large jagged scar on his belly that I'd like to think he got in a youthful knife-fight, but is more likely from an appendix operation. He often leaves his shirt open to air (or maybe to display) the scar, and scratches it when deep in thought.

Don Armando has five sons and a daughter by various mothers. The sons now help him run the business, which is large and thriving. The Doro Aná Pumé are fond of Don Armando in a guarded way, referring to him as "*Otámui,*" or "Old One." He has real liking and respect for Trino, whom he always greets with a yell and a big thump on the back. Don Armando likes us too,

crazy though he may think us, and everything the ranch has he offers us freely with charming, antique Latin courtesy.

His son Chi-chi, around 40, is nicknamed "*Gordo*," or Fatty, for his noble belly. Chi-chi loves food and will go to any lengths to get it, including following women around the kitchen, snatching bites, offering advice, and getting in the way. When he leaves his wife home at the ranch, he letches after girls on the street like a teenager. In many ways he really is like a big kid, but at his job of buying, selling, and transporting ranch goods, he has no equal.

Moraima, his wife, is about 23. Usually the only woman here, she somehow manages to keep the house and grounds clean, the clothes laundered, the small animals fed and sheltered, the store running, her baby girl cleaned and entertained, and the whole enterprise fed on the best-cooked *comida criolla* this side of the Apure river. Moraima is medium height with flawless, creamy brown skin, flyaway black hair, clear brown eyes, and generous Caribbean lips. When around strangers she is very matronly and proper, but the longer I know her the more I can discern a noisy, fun-loving virago underneath.

A good example of her dual personality was her reaction to Daniel's beating of Lu; what I mistook for apathy was inward anger carefully masked in the presence of an untrustworthy neighbor. In our private moments I've given her a couple packs of my birth control pills to try out, and we've had long talks about reproduction and health. I now feel easy helping her chop vegetables, wash dishes, or chase cows out of the garden.

Amanda, her 2-year-old daughter, has her mother's smooth-skinned beauty and her father's comical rolling walk. She is a big, healthy girl, growing up in an atmosphere any toddler would envy, full of animals, music, food, dirt, and any number of adoring grownups. Amanda grabs at the world with both fists and fears nothing but boredom.

Don Paco, Don Armando's eldest son, is a weatherbeaten cowboy of about 50 with a secret heartbreak, allegedly an estranged wife. His face is handsome, seamed with wrinkles and always shadowed by his old hat. I love coming across him on his pretty gray mare Bailarina (or "ballet dancer"), his sandalled feet dangling, a hand-rolled cigarette between his lips . . . Paco makes the Marlboro Men on the billboards at home look like a bunch of overfed milquetoasts. Strangely, he's very well read; he's traveled the world as a merchant marine sailor, and knows the U.S. electoral system better than I do.

Ronald, Don Armando's youngest son, is about 18 years old and being groomed to take over the ranch. He is rarely goofy and has no girlfriend—no time for it, probably. He is very tall and slender, with a girlishly pretty face, the hooked Aguilar nose, and a lively curiosity—he's always peppering us with questions about the States. I think we have a strong future friend in him.

These people form the heart of this beautiful ranch, around which various criollo and Pumé neighbors and workers orbit. It's a well-run place, a comfortable, busy place. Though it's a little more like home to me than Doro Aná, taken by itself Hato San Jacinto is still colorful and strange at times, a real Venezuelan up-country outfit.

Right now, it's quiet and sunny, the morning wind stirring the sparkling fronds of the stately coconut palms. Moraima is playing the radio and talking to Amanda while she sweeps the kitchen, and Ronald, out of boredom, is chasing the chickens. Sometimes Moraima plays tapes of *joropo*, the traditional ballads of the llaneran cowboys. She knows every tape by heart and sing-shouts along with them enthusiastically, and usually in tune.

The bittersweet sound of the harp and the plaintive voices will forever conjure up the Spanish part of the llanos for me—the leather of bridle and saddle, the flies, the sweet gray cows and their black calves, the spicy, salty food, the sweat, the tobacco, the liquor. Joropo is the best music in the world to drink to, whether you want a happy, noisy drunk, a brawling drunk, or a maudlin drunk.

7/29/93   All the ranchers have gone to town except Ronald, Moraima, little Amanda, a Pumé cowboy named Emilio, and me. Yesterday began with Moraima's cousin pedaling up with a huge sackful of white seed corn on his bicycle basket. We all sat out on the back porch with beers and shucked, scraped, and ground the sweet, hard kernels. Moraima put the mush in a bucket and mixed it with oil, milk, sugar, and salt. She ended up covered in batter up to her elbows, and bits splattered on her jeans and clung to her dark, frizzy hair.

After heating up a special griddle on the fire, she smeared oil on it with a corn husk and spent the next couple hours ladling batter onto the griddle and flipping *cachapas*, or corn cakes— they were a deep golden brown and over a foot in diameter. I watched and helped with the dishes while all of us gulped down beers, including Amanda. From time to time Moraima tore off a steaming, fragrant hunk of cachapa and pushed it at me, urging

"*Prueba-la!*" ("Try it!"). I thought of Rusty and Chuck boiling roots in Doro Aná while I munched, my cheeks bulging.

During a huge thunderstorm in the afternoon everyone sat on the front porch, drank more beer, and shouted at each other over joropo music on the radio. As it got dark I lay in my hammock, but I heard a couple of other men arrive and Moraima changed the joropo for raunchy dance music. The whooping, whistling, and roaring laughter eventually drew me out of my room like a magnet; Moraima and her cousin were two-stepping nimbly amid huge pyramids of beer cans. The Pumé cowboy and I strobed the couple with our flashlights to create a discotheque ambiance.

After a few hours and more beer I allowed myself to be badgered into dancing with young Ronald. Moraima's cousin, the self-appointed commentator and deejay, provided raucous encouragement, enthusing about my "modern style" of dancing. As most of my dance experience consists of punk-style slamming, I probably looked to them like I was having an epileptic fit.

After I'd staggered back into my room, the party continued unabated; I could hear the shuffling, slapping, and thumping of dancing feet get faster and faster. As I swung drunkenly in my hammock, fading into a sodden slumber, I overheard Ronald complaining to Moraima outside my window: "She dances way too crazy for me! I'd be *scared* to dance with her again . . . !"

This morning as I wandered out to pee I was impressed, despite my familiarity with the aftermaths of a thousand college parties; the porch looked like a battlefield in the mandarin orange rays of the rising sun. Chairs and stools lay tipped over in pools of beer, muddy footprints danced silently over the concrete, and beer cans and cigarette butts drifted like snow over every horizontal surface. The little tape player stood crookedly in the midst of it all like a monument to some obscure deity of drunken debauch.

8/4/93   Rusty and Chuck accompanied me as far as San Fernando in order to help me get my paperwork in order. We set out from the ranch two days ago in the windy predawn darkness. Moraima, who'd thoughtfully gotten up to fix us a big breakfast of arepas filled with spiced beef and peppers, stood sleepily in the dark doorway, her hair tousled, as we dragged our bags and packs out onto the porch. I gave her a clumsy kiss goodbye and we shouldered our packs and carefully felt our way through the dark down to the waiting boat. We loaded the bags, climbed in, and Ronald crossed himself as Pedro started the motor. As we eased out of the inlet onto the main body of the river, we could see it was flowing very deep and fast, and with the motor's help we sped east on the muscular back of the current.

It rained gently on us for an hour. Dawn was very gradual, the sky turning from dark slate gray to a diffuse, silvery lavender leaking slowly up from the eastern horizon. As it grew lighter the rain stopped, and occasionally the sky would coyly lift its skirt of dark clouds to reveal a lacy slip of glowing rosy orange. But the clouds always settled back down again, and we slid along in sleepy silence through a pearly, dim morning. The animals were chilly and drowsy, and only a few lonely great blue herons floated slowly through the trees along the banks.

As the sky lightened and the air warmed, we could see large green parrots lounging in the trees. Their livelier little cousins flew over us, always in pairs, chattering and patting the air with quick little wingbeats. Some of my favorites, whom we've dubbed the dinosaur birds, sat on branches with their wings spread to dry in the milky sunlight. They are glossy black birds about the size of an American robin with long tails and appealing faces, all beady clever eye and thick beak with a calloused area of skin around the nostril. They look like tiny, feathered Protoceratops. There are lots of them in Doro Aná, where they sit in the trees and serenade us with queer, whizzing calls, and in San Fernando, where they mob the plaza and beg clownishly for crumbs.

I felt deeply at peace as we floated downriver. I knew I was seeing this beautiful river, and the little Pumé and criollo houses on its banks, for perhaps the last time. But the part of me that was crying stayed deeply buried, and another, stronger part said, I'm going home now, the end is just as important as the beginning. And the llanos, with its animals, plants, and people, its fires and its rainbows, will stretch in all its colors in me forever. I feel huge inside: the wind blows through the ripening grassheads and over huge curving sand dunes, the ibises croak as they fly through my heart.

8/7/93   After only one day in town Rusty and Chuck have had to return to the ranch, as it was the only ride available for weeks. We said a hurried goodbye and I watched them climb onto a tiny bus that would carry them back to La Lechuga. Now that they've gone I feel empty and alone, and I've kept myself busy trying to make sure all my immigration paperwork and airline tickets are in order. Tonight is my last night on the llanos.

I walked over the town bridge this evening and watched the Rio Apure flow underneath me like an anaconda of molten pewter. It coiled sluggishly in the setting sun, festooned with white water lilies. Two cormorants paddled in the current, their bodies and tails under water, their sleek black heads and necks snaking up insolently to look at me. I remembered how rich and delicious their dark meat is.

As poor squatters camped on the riverbank started fires to cook the turtles and cayman they'd just caught, I leaned on my elbows and remembered a sunset walk Rusty and I had made hand-in-hand along this bank a year and a half ago. A young, scruffy criollo teenager had pedaled slowly past us on his bike, flashing us his white teeth in a smile. "*Una tierra bonita, verdad?*" his voice had floated back to us through the still evening air. "Yes," we'd called after him, "it is a beautiful land."

8/8/93   My bus trip back to the capital began badly, with a patrol of National Guard soldiers stopping us at the Apure state border and ordering everyone off the bus. They've been cracking down on Colombian terrorists and are running random checks on all public transport. We stood around uneasily while two soldiers poked around our bags. One of them looked up sharply when he saw my three huge military-surplus duffle bags. "Whose are these?" he shouted at the bus driver, who shrugged.

I stepped forward and a soldier leveled the muzzle of his automatic weapon at my belly. "They're mine," I said in a shaky voice. "They're full of Indian artifacts." The soldier with his gun on me demanded my passport and I handed it over. For some reason (quite possibly he couldn't read), he said nothing about my expired visa. Eventually we were allowed back onto the bus and I collapsed into my seat, trembling.

As we drove through the countryside the deeply flooded pastures on either side of the road were dotted with the black, boxy shapes of water buffalo wading and grazing in the mists. In the trees along the road were vast flocks of waterfowl, including cormorants, black egrets, blue herons, white egrets, black ibis, green ibis, and the largest groups of scarlet ibis I've ever seen. These birds are so red they're unearthly; when they take flight in numbers and the light glows through their scarlet wings, they look like flying sprays of molten lava. Seeing them is always startling, like a sharp sensation of physical pleasure.

As we drove north, we climbed through little mountain towns. We could now see traces of a hurricane, which obviously hadn't come as far south as San Fernando but explained the large flocks of birds disturbed from their normal roosting grounds. The Caribbean islands and the northern half of the country, according to the newspapers, had been badly hit the night before. We passed swollen, rust-red rivers writhing dangerously in their beds, and higher up the banks dead grass and trees, all swept in the same direction, showed where the flood had peaked hours before. Many small fields and gardens on the riverbank had been destroyed, the

plantain and corn plants lying strewn like sodden corpses in the
red mud.

The river was still very violent, and I could tell who hadn't lost
anything by the cheerful throngs gathered in the little restaurants
to drink beer and gawk at the seething waters below. By contrast,
riverbank dwellers stood on the banks near their flooded homes,
tiredly surveying their ruined fields, soaked houses, and the furniture hastily piled in the mud in their yards.

We were lucky not to have been caught in the storm, but the
aftermath of huge mudslides blocking the highways was serious
enough. I've now been sitting in the bus station at Maracay for
hours, waiting for news about the road to Caracas. The joropo
music playing on the bus radio consoles me a little; it's the song
about the dawn, my favorite. I've been unable to discover this
singer's name, and it makes the song more precious to me, that I
can only trust to blind chance to hear it.

8/18/93   I'm sitting in J.F.K. airport, my eyelids raw, hands twitching, trying to come down from my last frantic hours in Venezuela. After staying the night in Maracay with our friends, Dr. Otto Fornés and his wife Margarita, I reboarded the bus, which crept the few miles to Caracas over three hours, avoiding the slews of clay mud that had inundated the highway.

In Caracas I spent the night with Flor Chavez, the sister of a Spanish teacher in Albuquerque, and her family. They kindly sent me off to the airport at 4:30 the next morning, loaded up with my last cup of dark, sweet Venezuelan coffee. In the taxi I noticed with faint dismay that after cab fare I would have almost no money left.

After confirming my ticket and checking my enormous bags, I was stopped at the immigration checkpoint. The officials told me the letter I'd been given by their office in San Fernando, which was supposedly my pass out of the country, was invalid. I would have to somehow get my bags out of check, travel the thirty miles back into the capital, and wait ten more days for the paperwork to go through. My airline ticket, of course, was going to be sacrificed.

During my frantic attempts to argue with the immigration officials and retrieve my baggage, someone stole a small bag I'd been carrying, which had been full of developed rolls of film, all priceless, irreplaceable data and personal photos. About 1,000 exposures in total.

After five days with next to no food or sleep and still weakened by anemia from the hookworm, this disastrous theft sent me abruptly over the edge. Banging my forehead on the countertop, I howled and sobbed. This deeply impressed the airline personnel, and a matronly young woman grabbed me by the elbow and hustled me to the Lost and Found Department to report the lost bag.

While I was stammering out a description, the baggage claim man came racing over, shouting, "I've fixed it! She can leave! But she's gotta go *right now*, the plane's taking off!" I gave up on the lost bag and fled for the gate after thanking the young woman and the baggage claim man, who'd walked over to the immigration post and browbeaten the sullen officials into letting me go.

On the way to New York I slumped in the airplane seat and leaked slow tears of relief, anger, and exhaustion for hour after hour. A kindly Caraqueña, noticing me, chatted to me in Spanish and English to distract me. She made sure I ate all my breakfast and that I filled out my customs form correctly.

When we separated in the airport I hugged her and kissed her fragrant powdered cheek, and all of Venezuela, goodbye. Then I turned and walked alone down the long, echoing hallway. Turning out my pockets, I dug out my last $1.98 and laughed unbelievingly as I headed for home.

Epilogue

Rusty arrived home in late October of 1993 with the latest news of the Doro Aná Pumé.

Young Carmen Cartoria and Gusha both had their babies with little trouble, and now there are yet two *more* little girls in the community.

Pedro Julio's elder wife, Amelia, was pregnant in October and has since given birth. Her daughter, Marina, was also pregnant and has had her first baby by her slipshod husband, Marcos Pala.

Juana Trina's tiny Domana, whom we saved from death by a mysterious illness in July of 1992, fell ill with pneumonia in a neighboring camp shortly after Rusty and Chuck returned from San Fernando. Juana Trina waited too long before seeking help, and the little girl lost the fight for her life almost exactly one year after her first miraculous recovery.

My special daughter Ana, never a strong baby, fell ill in August and Rusty struggled to save her for several weeks. She pulled through with his help, that time.

Unlike my sendoff, which (characteristic of Pumé women) had been quiet, Rusty and Chuck's leave-taking was very emotional. All the men accompanied them to the ranch to help them carry their baggage. When it came time to say goodbye, the men did something very unusual; they laid hands on Rusty, as they told him it was important for him to return. Rusty unsuccessfully fought back the tears.

But before he'd left camp, Lucrecia had approached him and took hold of Rusty's arm. "Make sure when you come back, that your wife comes with you," she urged.

We are currently at work coding the data we took on the Pumé into computers, and Rusty's dissertation is under way. Our reports to the Venezuelan government concerning Pumé land rights and health are also in progress.

I have decided to pursue a Ph.D. in archaeology at Southern Methodist University. As I strain my eyes late at night poring over endless piles of articles, or banging away at the keyboard in a desperate race to finish a paper, I sometimes reward myself with tiny reminiscences of Venezuela, and of our lives with the Pumé. They understand we will be coming back as soon as we can. I can picture them asking each other around the tohé fires, "What could be taking them so long?"

Appendix A

A

areáh—to weave

adóh—and, in addition to

agurí—to defecate

aí—mother

aibuí—mother's sister

ajimúi—big brother

akú—stomach, belly

amí—big sister

ámui—father

aná—big, large

anyikuí—little sister

anyikui tohé—"little sister tohé," or the women's solo form of tohé, where one woman sings without assistance all night

arí—cayman crocodile (also see Appendix D)

B

bai—manioc, sweet or bitter (also see Appendix C)

bai eró—fermented drink made from manioc

bai uí—boiled liquid byproduct from processing bitter manioc; in taste, it is similar to hot chocolate

Ba kodí—I'm going away.

Bedawí—Wake up!

bi—a plant cultivated for fish poison; also called barbasco in Spanish (also see Appendix C)

bo—a baby human being

bobuí—weaving material made from the baby form of the moriche palm (also see Appendix C). The young leaf is folded and the stiff midrib is stripped out. Bobuí is used for rougher weaving, mostly mats.

bomái—pregnant

buá—deer (also see Appendix D)

buí—small; also used to describe the young of animals

buíchineh—a little, or a little bit

burí—sleeping hammock

C

chi—to peel or strip

chiá—to wash away or rinse

chinakarú—an edible, nutlike pod that grows on trees by the creek; usually in season May–July (also see Appendix C)

chirí—the open savanna

chirurí—a small edible lizard (also see Appendix D)

chiyokodé—the man's ceremonial rattle, made out of a hollowed gourd that is filled with tiny pebbles and ornamentally carved. These sacred rattles are used during tohé and are not supposed to see the light of day.

chokuí—a small edible wild root, usually in season July–September (also see Appendix C)

chuanyí/chuaméh—fierce, stubborn, ferocious. The -nyí suffix indicates a female subject, the -méh suffix a male subject.

chúchu—a woman's breast

cuiná—stingray common to South American freshwater habitats. Its flesh is edible and the tiny barbed point on its stinging tail (called the cuiná buí) is removed by the Pumé to use as a piercer

in various strengthening, disciplining, and curing ceremonies
(also see Appendix D).

D

dapué—a very common edible fish. It is a carnivore with needlelike teeth that can reach a length of about 14 inches (also see
Appendix D).

-deh—the negative suffix. Can be attached to the end of either
verbs, adverbs, and adjectives to negate them.

doh—sun; can also denote one day

doró—creek or stream

Doro Aná—Big Creek, the savanna community we worked in

E

eá—to wish or want; in rare contexts, to love or desire

edé—a large, golden-fleshed domesticated squash, also known to
the Spanish as *auyama*

G

gabaechó—an edible fruit; usually in season June–August (also see
Appendix C)

gitó—pain or ache

Gito má—the Region of Pain, a Pumé euphemism for the world in
which we live

go—weaving material made from the soft inner membrane of the
baby leaf of the moriche palm. Go is finer than bobuí and is
used for fine basketry, loincloths, and string.

go-aburé—the women's loincloth, made of go dyed red. The go is
tied around the hips using a small belt, usually of cotton.

gochí—to strip the inner membrane from the baby moriche palm
leaf

gotaiyó—basket or purse made of go

gupenéh—moon; can also mean month

gwa—to have, to possess

H

Há wu!—Go for it, take it!

habí—daughter

hamboá—gone, dead, emptied

handí—in this way; can also mean, this many; as a question, it can mean, Is that so?

hatchí—far away; can also be used to mean, Get out of here!

hiámui—mother's father; also used to address certain spirits or animals who are seen by the Pumé as standing in that spiritual relationship to them

hii—mosquito net. Normally made by the women out of meticulously sewn patches of cloth, as the Pumé cannot obtain netting.

ho—house or building

Hu!—Sic 'em! Go get 'em!

hudí—mature moriche palm leaf, usually used for thatching (also see Appendix C)

hurutú—tired, footsore

I

iéh—female

igurú—the savanna armadillo (also see Appendix D)

ipurimechá—the tegu lizard, whose flesh is edible. Often reaches a length of 24–30 inches (also see Appendix D).

K

ka—my, mine

kéhinyi/kémeh—named or called. The -nyi suffix indicates a female subject, the -meh suffix a male subject.

keramuí—brother-in-law

keranyí—sister-in-law

kodí—me, I

kondechará—"fire chair," indicating any ground-moving, motorized vehicle; rare use for airplane

Kumanyí—the Creatress, the principal deity in Pumé mythology

kuyú—edible grublike larvae of a certain palm beetle (also see Appendix D)

M

maná—to come or arrive

Manawú—Come here!

Manabí—Come back!

menéh—you (singular and plural)

mishotóh—plant used in fish poisoning (also see Appendix C)

moéh—hot, ripe, as in fruit. Can also mean pregnant, or indicate that labor contractions are imminent.

N

na—your, yours

nanú—the tree (and its seeds) that produces the basic component of Pumé ceremonial hallucinogenic snuff (also see Appendix C)

ngoitóh—an edible fruit, usually in season February–April (also see Appendix C)

ngoipá—to write or draw

Ngoipawú—Write it down! Get it on paper!

niyatéh—the metal lance, usually leaf-shaped, that is used in the hunting of large mammals

niwéi—people of European descent; more generally, white foreigner. Carries a mildly insulting meaning.

niwí—ecstatic, in the religious or spirit-possessed sense; may also mean drunk

no indanéh—endless, an infinite quantity

nyoní—two, both

Nyuwú—Speak! Say it!

nyurí—menstruation (noun) or menstruating (verb)

nyurihó—menstruation hut or shelter

nyuritái—menstruation dish

O

oi—male

onikorí—an edible fruit and the tree it grows on; usually in season April–June (also see Appendix C)

Otámui—Old Man, or Old Granddad. An affectionate term for an old man who is not closely related to you.

Ote tí—The Old Ones, or Ancestors. They are represented in each Pumé community by a group of small rocks and sometimes a carved or ceramic animal-shaped figurine. These objects are kept, usually in the house of the healer, in a cloth sack and are brought out for each tohé ceremony.

P

-pa—suffix meaning, to make or to do; can also be used to indicate future tense

paintó—the woven fire fan that also serves as a bug swatter, food preparation platform, and household broom

pará—an edible wild root; usually in season April–November (also see Appendix C)

piyí—there is, or there are; can also mean immediacy (time) or proximity (location)

puá—songbird, or small bird in general

Pumé—The People, or Family. Usually means the language and cultural group of the Pumé, but can be extended to mean any American Indian group. Can also mean the family of a particular individual.

Pumé máeh—the Pumé tongue or language

pundichará—an edible fish (also see Appendix D)

R

-ru—suffix meaning there, in that place

rupéh—a place or location

T

ta—a lagoon or small lake

Ta Aná—the Big Lagoon, located about 3/4 mile east of Doro Aná. The criollo family of Moleto lives on the banks in the dry season, and the Doro Aná Pumé establish temporary fishing camps there.

tabadá—the woven floor mat. Is recorded in the ethnographic literature as serving as a cape or cloak prior to the introduction of cloth to the Pumé.

tai—bowl made of half of a hollowed-out gourd

taiyó—large basket made for rough work, like carrying wood or roots

tambái—flat cake made of grated, dried, and sifted bitter manioc. Called cassava in Spanish, these cakes are common in cities and smaller indigenous communities across South America.

taranyuná—the Pumé deer-hunting hat. It is formed of a woven cap, into which is inserted a carved wooden stork's head that has been charred black. The cap is covered in black cloth.

taréh—mosquitoes

tikirí—children's toy

tochó—an edible seed whose tree grows along the creekbed; usually in season June–August (also see Appendix C)

toh kaereah tóh—the Pumé face-painting stick. Men carve intricate patterns onto the surface of finger-sized sticks, which are coated with the juice of a red seedpod (onoto). The surface "stamps" the design onto the face. These sticks are falling out of use with the advent of lipstick in the trade network.

toh pundéh—a leaf used as a medicine for female complaints, and as a red dye for the women's loincloth (also see Appendix C) *toh yowa réh*—a possumlike marsupial predator, not edible (also see Appendix D)

tohé—the all-night ceremony involving dancing, singing, and curing practices. Tohé is held up to four times a week in the wet season.

Tohé ngwá—There's tohé tonight.

topaté—small, wooden delousing tool

toréh—a slim metal shovel, about 8 inches by 4 inches, favored by the Pumé women for root-digging. The shovel is usually obtained by trade with river Pumé. It is called a *chicora* in Spanish.

tuípa—a mildly hallucinogenic root; used by the Pumé to mediate the violent effects of nanú (also see Appendix C)

tuú—an edible root; usually in season April–May (also see Appendix C)

U

uapá—to be afraid

uí—water

Uí Aná—the Big Water, or the ocean

Uí Aná Rupéh—the country across the ocean. Can mean any distant region.

uihurúhuda—praying mantis

uín—conception

uin déh toh—contraceptive plant (also see Appendix C)

uin chiá toh—abortifacient plant (also see Appendix C)

uringwá—a medicinal plant that acts like heating rub when crushed and rubbed on the body (also see Appendix C)

W

-wu—suffix indicating the imperative tense

Y

yakará—a large edible fish; called *pavon* in Spanish, rainbow bass in English (also see Appendix D)

yegupái—medium-sized edible fish (also see Appendix D)

yipái—an edible wild root, the most important to the Pumé wet season diet; usually in season June–December (also see Appendix C)

Appendix B

A

alpargata—men's sandals common in the llanos, made of thin tire soles and woven cloth uppers

arepa—a corn flour (masa) patty or dumpling that is boiled, steamed or fried; used commonly as bread with the llaneran meal, or as a bun for sandwiches

B

batido—a drink made of chilled fruit, sugar, and water or milk, which are beaten together in a blender

bolívar—the standard unit of money in Venezuela, named after the Liberator Simon Bolívar; the bolívar is currently valued at about one American penny

bonita/-o—pretty, lovely

C

caceroler—to stage a protest by whacking on a casserole dish or pot with a spoon; a common method of urban demonstration that can be done safely from your kitchen window

cachapa—a large corn pancake made with ground kernels, milk, oil, and sugar; often serves as a wrapping for cheese or meat *café con leche*—"coffee with milk"; can mean either the beverage or the ethnic mix of the Venezuelan population

caiman—the South American crocodile (also see Appendix D)

caño—creek or stream and the incised bed through which it runs

capitán—"captain"; locally meant as the spokesperson for a Pumé community. The Pumé capitan translates, interprets, and advises for his people, but has no real authority.

Carnaval—the boisterous Catholic holiday that precedes Lent, known more commonly in the United States by the French term, Mardi Gras

castellano—the South American term for the Spanish language, taught in U.S. schools as Español

catalina—a sweet, soft brown molasses cookie, popular with Venezuelan children

chinchorro—literally, "fishing net"; in Venezuela the word means the sleeping hammock

comida—food or meal

criolla/-o—describes a mix of Indian and Spanish ancestry. The ranching people of the llanos are all criollos, with varying degrees of Caribbean blood as well.

G

ganado—cattle

ganadero—a cowboy or rancher

guapa/-o—cute, good-looking

Guardia Nacional—"National Guard"; the Venezuelan equivalent of the Army

J

joropo—Venezuelan cowboy music, whose instruments usually include a small guitar or cuatro, maracas or rattles, and most notably, the harp, an antique form brought over from Spain. Both men and women sing a special form of verse lyric, whose subjects may include love, revenge, cowboy life, or patriotism.

L

llanos—savanna, or grassland. The Venezuelan llanos is located in a belt across the center of the country, in the basin of the Orinoco River.

M

machete—the swordlike tool used to chop at vegetation all over South America, Africa, and Asia

manteca—oil

mosquitero—mosquito net. In South America, it is a tentlike structure, made of breathable cotton, that can be strung up along with the hammock in any setting.

P

paludismo—malaria

pan dulce—sweet, soft bread, usually flavored with star anise

patron—the boss of a ranch or farm. The patron is usually responsible for the well-being of his workers, whom he generally pays in food and goods, not in cash. He pays for all clothing and health care for his workers.

pixteca—a term originating in Peru for the South American equivalent of a body-snatcher or vampire. This person kidnaps children or helpless adults in order to kill or drug them and steal their organs, which are sold on the international black market. The practice has not been officially recognized by any government.

probar—to test, try, or try out. Prueba-la! = "Try that!"

R

río—river

S

Semana Santa—Holy Week, the week in the spring culminating in Easter Sunday

T

tierra—earth or land

V

verdad—truth. In question form, it means "Isn't it the truth?"

Appendix C

(alphabetical by Pumé term)

bai (Manihot esculenta)—manioc, bitter or sweet; an edible root (the only edible plant the savanna Pumé cultivate with success)

bi (Tephrosia cinapou)—a fish-poisoning agent cultivated by the *Pumé* (also known as *barbasco*)

chinakarú (Panopsis rubescens)—a wild, edible nut

chokuí (Myrosma cannifolia)—a wild, edible bulb

gabaechó (Covepia padaensis)—a sweet, crumbly wild fruit

hudí/bobuí/go (Mauritia flexuosa)—the moriche palm tree

mángo (Mangifera indica)—common mango, introduced from Asia, cultivated without much success by the savanna Pumé

mishotóh (not yet identified)—A fish-poisoning agent that grows in the wild

nanú (Anadenanthera peregrina)—a powerful hallucinogen collected in the wild

ngoitóh (Hymenaea courbaril)—a hard-shelled wild fruit

onikorí (Licania spp.)—sweet, greasy-fleshed fruit that is cultivated by the criollos on the river *pará (Dioscurea* spp.*)*—edible wild tuber, related to the sweet potato

tochó (Macrolobium multijugatum)—an edible wild seed

topundéh (Arrabidaea chica)—a women's medicinal herb that grows in the wild

tuípa (Banisteriopsis spp.*)*—a mild hallucinogen that is cultivated by the Pumé

tuú (Heliconia psittacorum)—an edible wild root

uindétoh (not yet identified)—a women's contraceptive herb

uin chiá toh (not yet identified)—an abortifacient

uringwá (not yet identified)—medicinal herb that is collected in the wild

yipái (Dracontium margaritae)—a staple edible root collected in the wild

Appendix D

(alphabetical by common English term; Pumé term in bold-
face and italics)

anteater, arboreal—*Temandua tetradactyla*, **tuchupí**

anteater, giant—*Myrmecophaga tridactyla*, **arigurí**

armadillo (seven-banded)—*Dasypus sabanicola*, **igurú**

assassin bug—*Tyriatoma* spp.

barn owl—*Tyto alba*, **hututú**

bass, rainbow—*Cichla ocellaris*, **yakará**

beetle, palm—*Rhincophorus* spp., **kuyú**

boa constrictor—*Boa constrictor*, **po**

capybara—*Hydrochaeris hydrochaeris*, **chidó**

caracara—*Polyborus plancus*, **tené**

cayman—*Caiman crocodilus*, **arí**

cichlid (fish)—*Geophagus daemon*, **pundichará**

coral snake—*Micrurus isozonus*, **daiyapó**

cormorant—*Phalacrocorax olivaceus*, **hewé**

deer, brocket—*Mazama americana*, **buá**

deer, white-tailed—*Odocoileus virginianus*, **buá yatechiá**

dolphin, freshwater—*Inia geoffrensis*, **oibí**

dove—*Zenaida auriculata*, **hotokó**

egret, cattle—*Egretta thula*, **hokará**

heron, blue—*Ardea herodias*, **andurá**
hoatzin—*Opisthocomus hoazin*
ibis, scarlet—*Edocimus ruber*, **corocoró**
jaguar—*Panthera onca*, **guantió**
lizard, racerunner—various spp., **chirurí**
macaw, military—*Ara macao*
mosquito—*Anopheles* spp., **taréh**
opossum, thick-tailed—*Lutreolina crassicaudata*, **toh yowa réh**
parrot, small yellowhead—*Amazona ochrocephala*, **geregeré**
pirhana—*Serrasalmus notatus*, **apéi**
rabbit, cottontail—*Sylvilagus flondanus*, **tapará**
pit viper—*Bothrops atrox*, **po chiá**
rattlesnake—*Crotalus durissus*, **chiagodé**
stingray—*Dasytis guttata*, **cuiná**
tapir—*Tapirus terrestris*, **hoyéi**
tegu—*Tupinambis teguixin*, **ipurimechá**
tortoise—*Geochelone carbonaria*, **apatí**
trahira (fish)—*Hoplias malabaricus*, **dapué**
turtle—*Podocnemis unifilis*, **chiridamé**

FURTHER READING

Anderson, Barbara Gallatin
  1991. *First Fieldwork: The Misadventures of an Anthropologist.* Prospect Heights, IL: Waveland Press.

Branch, Hilary Dunsterville
  1993. *Venezuela.* Bucks, England: Chalfont St. Peters Press.

Eisenberg, John F.
  1989. *Mammals of the Neotropics: The Northern Neotropics, Vol. 1.* Chicago: University of Chicago Press.

Hilton, Charles E.
  1997. "Comparative locomotor kinematics and kinetics in two contemporary hominid groups: sedentary Americans and mobile Venezuelan foragers." (Ph.D. diss., University of New Mexico).

Levi-Straus, Claude
  1967. *Tristes Tropiques.* New York: Atheneum Press.

Lyon, Patricia
  1985. *Native South Americans: Ethnology of the Least Known Continent.* Prospect Heights, IL: Waveland Press.

Mitrani, Philippe
  1988. Los Pumé (Yaruro). In *Los aborígenes de Venezuela,*

vol. 2: *Etnología contempor·nea*, ed. W. Coppens and B. Escalante (Fundación La Salle de Ciencias Naturales, Instituto Caribe de Antropología y Sociología. Caracas: Monte Avila Editores).

Petrullo, Vincent M.
1939. The Yaruros of the Capanaparo River, Venezuela. In *Bureau of American Ethnology Bulletin* 123, Anthropology Papers No. 11 (Washington, DC: U.S. Government Printing Office).

Thomas, Elizabeth Marshall
1959. *The Harmless People*. New York: Vintage Books.

Ward, Martha Coonfield
1989. *Nest in the Wind: Adventures in Anthropology on a Tropical Island*. Prospect Heights, IL: Waveland Press.

Wilbert, Johannes, and Karin Simoneau, eds.
1990. *Folk Literature of the Yaruro Indians*. Los Angeles: University of California Press, Latin America Publications.